WORL

BIBLE TRAINING CENTER

MURRIETA · CALIFORNIA

TRAINING BELIEVERS TO MOVE WITH THE WORD & THE SPIRIT

FOR MORE INFO OR TO SUBMIT AN APPLICATION ONLINE, GO TO

WWW.WHBTC.ORG

OR CONTACT OUR OFFICE AT (951) 696-9258, EXT. 202

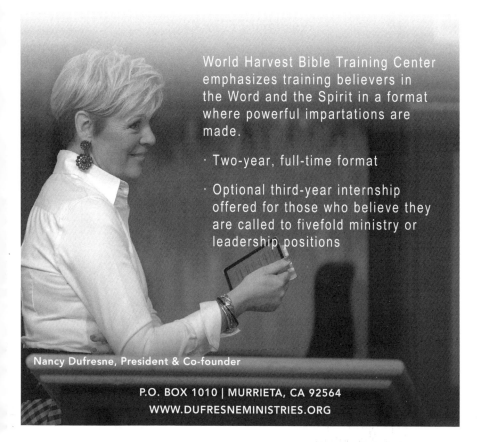

World Harvest Bible Training Center emphasizes training believers in the Word and the Spirit in a format where powerful impartations are made.

· Two-year, full-time format

· Optional third-year internship offered for those who believe they are called to fivefold ministry or leadership positions

Nancy Dufresne, President & Co-founder

P.O. BOX 1010 | MURRIETA, CA 92564
WWW.DUFRESNEMINISTRIES.ORG

Books by Nancy Dufresne

Daily Healing Bread From God's Table

His Presence Shall Be My Dwelling Place

The Healer Divine

Victory in the Name

*There Came a Sound From Heaven:
The Life Story of Dr. Ed Dufresne*

Visitations From God

Responding to the Holy Spirit

God: The Revealer of Secrets

A Supernatural Prayer Life

Causes

I Have a Supply

*Fit for the Master's Use:
A Handbook for Raising Godly Children*

A Sound, Disciplined Mind

Knowing Your Measure of Faith

The Greatness of God's Power

Peace: Living Free From Worry

An Apostle of the Anointing:
A Biography of Dr. Ed Dufresne

Victory Over Grief & Sorrow

Answer It!

The Price of the Double Portion Anointing

Worship

Love: The Great Quest

Books in Spanish

Pan Diario de Sanidad de la Mesa de Dios
(Spanish edition of *Daily Healing Bread*)

Contents

Dedication.. ix

Introduction... xi

1. Follow the Spirit... 13

2. The Inward Witness.. 19

3. The Inward Witness Defined.................................... 25

4. It's Easy To Follow the Spirit................................. 37

5. Immediately Obey Your Spirit................................ 53

6. Don't Get in a Ditch – Stay Balanced.................... 57

7. Don't Wreck Your Faith... 67

8. You Have an Unction... 71

9. The Profit of the Spirit.. 81

10. The Advantage the Spirit Gives............................. 89

11. Your Measure of Faith... 97

12. Ministering by the Spirit....................................... 103

13. Developing Your Spirit... 111

14. Following the Holy Spirit Regarding...

   What To Believe For 119

   Healing 121

   Finances 122

   The Will of God 125

   Prayer 128

15. In Closing 131

Prayer of Salvation 133

How To Be Filled With the Holy Spirit 135

Prayer To Receive the Holy Spirit 139

Dedication

This book is lovingly dedicated to the man with whom I shared almost 30 years of my life. He was my Bible school, my example, and the man I loved, Dr. Ed Dufresne.

He taught me, as well as the Body of Christ, to move with the Word and the Spirit.

He was my foremost example in following the Holy Spirit.

Introduction

One of the great privileges of every believer is to have the indwelling Presence of the Holy Spirit. He has left Heaven to dwell in the believer, making us His home.

He has come to be our ever-present companion, to guide and lead us in this journey we are on and in this race we are running.

First John 4:4 tells us, *"...greater is he that is in you, than he that is in the world."* Since the Greater One is in us, our life should reflect His greatness in every way.

Before we were born again, we were sentenced to live this life only by what *we* know, but because of the Word and the Spirit within, we now have the privilege of living by what *God* knows.

The Spirit of God has come to help the Church fulfill the will of God in the earth. He will teach, guide, and lead us in carrying out God's great work, but we must learn to recognize and follow His leading.

God will guide us through:

1) The inward witness

2) The voice of our spirit

3) The authoritative voice of the Holy Spirit

4) Other ways – prophecy, visions, dreams

The primary and foremost way God leads the believer is through the inward witness. So, with this in mind, this book focuses on learning how to follow the Holy Spirit through the inward witness.

The Holy Spirit endeavors to lead every believer through the inward witness, but many don't recognize it and don't know to follow it.

I trust that through this book, many will come to better recognize and follow the leading of the Spirit.

*Note: for further study on the ways God guides, I recommend *How You Can Be Led by the Spirit* by Kenneth E. Hagin.

Chapter 1

Follow the Spirit

"If you can teach people to follow their spirit, you can help them in every arena of life." These are words spoken by my spiritual father. He understood that our greatest help and success come by following our spirit.

As a pastor and a teacher of the Word, I have endeavored to teach people to follow their spirit, rather than to lean on the help and faith of others. At times of opposition, difficulty, and testing, someone else may not always be around to help you. But there is an ever-present Helper on the inside of you to help you at all times. The more we are aware of Him and yield to Him, the more help we will receive from Him.

Jesus told His disciples before He was crucified, *"...It is expedient* (advantageous) *for you that I go away: for if I go not away, the Comforter will not come unto you; but if I depart, I will send him unto you"* (John 16:7). Jesus said that it was for our advantage that He go and the Comforter, the Holy Spirit, come in His place.

To have the Holy Spirit within is advantageous for us; it gives us the advantage in every way and in every situation to have His divine help and guidance.

One of the greatest things is to know what to do – what to do when faced with decisions, what to do with our life, and what to do in the emergencies of life. One of the great advantages of having the Spirit within is He will lead us in what we're to do. He makes known to us the mind of God for our life and for the situations we face. This gives us the advantage over every enemy, over every circumstance, and over every situation. It is a privilege to have the Holy Spirit within who gives us the divine advantage.

Yet to benefit from this greater Comforter and Helper, we must learn to listen to Him and to follow and obey Him.

On one occasion, Jesus appeared to my spiritual father and said, "If you learn to follow My Spirit, I'll make you rich. I'm not opposed to My people being rich; I'm opposed to them being covetous." (Rich means having a full supply, having more than enough.)

Well, if following the Spirit will make you rich, bless you financially, then won't following the Spirit bless you in every other arena of life? Most certainly it will!

But notice the condition Jesus spoke with this – "IF you learn to follow My Spirit...." Our blessing is connected to how well we know and follow the leading of the Spirit.

I like what one pastor said, "God planned it, Jesus purchased it, but it's the Spirit who leads us into it." God planned total victory for us in every arena of life, and Jesus came and purchased that victory for us, but the Holy Spirit leads us into experiencing the victory God planned and Jesus purchased. Without the help of the Holy Spirit leading us, we would not experience all God planned and Jesus purchased for us. The more we learn to follow the Holy Spirit, the more victory we will experience in every arena of life.

Life in the Spirit

The emphasis for the New Testament believer is life in the Spirit. We are told in the New Testament to:

1) be filled with the Spirit (Eph. 5:18)

2) pray with the spirit (1 Cor. 14:15)

3) sing with the spirit (1 Cor. 14:15)

4) walk in the Spirit (Gal. 5:16 & 25)

It is our great privilege to be the temple of the Holy Ghost (1 Cor. 6:19). He dwells in us; we are the residency of the Holy Spirit.

Since God the Holy Ghost dwells in us, it gives us a great advantage in life in every way, but still we must learn to follow Him to benefit from His indwelling Presence.

To live in the Spirit means to be mindful of the Spirit within our spirit and to listen to and follow what He communicates to our spirit.

He'll Show Us Things To Come

JOHN 16:13-15
13 Howbeit when he, the Spirit of truth, is come, he will guide you into all truth: for he shall not speak of himself; but whatsoever he shall hear, that shall he speak: and he will shew you things to come.
14 He shall glorify me: for he shall receive of mine, and SHALL SHEW IT UNTO YOU.
15 All things that the Father hath are mine: therefore said I, that he shall take of mine, and SHALL SHEW IT UNTO YOU.

Notice in these three verses, Jesus told us three times that the Spirit would show us things. One of the great advantages of the Spirit dwelling within is that He will show us things to come. One reason this benefits us is so we can be prepared for what's ahead. But another reason He shows us things to come is because some of these things need our faith so that they can come to pass.

God's plan for our life will not come to pass automatically. The blessings that He has for our life will not come to pass automatically. The things God has for us need our faith so that they can come to pass. One of the things the Holy Spirit will show us is what God has for us in the future so that we can add our faith to it, and then God can bring it to pass. God needs our agreement to bring His will to pass in our life – our faith is our agreement.

The more sensitive we are to the Spirit within, the more we will see what He endeavors to show us.

The Word & The Spirit

In this era, God is raising up strong local churches that move with the Word and the Spirit.

The *Word* of God gives the *general* instruction that applies to and belongs to all of God's people. But the *Spirit* of God will lead us into the *specifics* about our life.

The Word tells us that God will supply all our needs (Phil. 4:19), but it doesn't tell us what job to take, what house to buy, or what city to live in – these are things the Spirit will lead us in. The Word tells us about marriage, but it doesn't tell us who to marry – the Spirit will lead us in this.

The Word speaks *generally* to all of God's people, but the Spirit leads us regarding the *specifics* of our life.

To experience total success, we need the Word and the Spirit. The Spirit works with the Word; He always leads us in line with God's Word. His leading will never violate the instruction of the Word, but will always be in agreement with it.

Chapter 2

The Inward Witness

Romans 8:14 reads, *"For as many as are led by the Spirit of God, they are the sons of God."* God is telling us that the sons of God are led by the Spirit of God. In this verse, God is promising to lead us by His Spirit.

God doesn't lead us by feelings or circumstances; He leads us by His Spirit. Some think that if a particular circumstance arises or if they have a certain feeling, that is God leading them. No, God leads us by His Spirit and not by feelings or circumstances that arise.

This verse shows us how the Spirit deals with us – He leads us. When making a decision, make sure you're being led and not driven. The Spirit leads us – He doesn't drive us. If something is driving you to do something, that's not the Spirit of God dealing with you, for He doesn't drive, He leads. The devil will try to drive people through fear, worry, doubt, jealousy, greed, etc., but God will not.

Since the Spirit leads, then He must be in front with you following. He will lead a particular direction, but it's up to you whether or not you follow His lead. You can follow His lead or not follow it – it's up to you. He won't force you, make you, or drive you. If you follow His lead, you'll be blessed. It's up to you. He doesn't force anyone to move into more blessing, but He will lead you into it if you're willing to follow Him there.

Anointed To Follow

Again, Romans 8:14 reads, *"For as many as are LED by the SPIRIT of God, they are the sons of God."* The Spirit is qualified and has the ability to be in the lead; He's anointed to lead. Sons are anointed to follow. God's children are not anointed to lead the Spirit, but to follow His lead.

It's dangerous to bypass the leading of the Spirit and try to take the lead position for our life ourselves. The Spirit of God knows the mind of God; He knows what God's will is for our life, and He will lead us in line with God's will. To disregard the Spirit's leading to follow our own lead will turn out badly for us. Our safety, our blessing, and our victory are in following the lead of the One who knows the mind of God for our life. He's anointed to lead; we're anointed to follow.

You Are a Spirit

God leads us by His Spirit; His Spirit communicates to our spirit what the will of God is, then we are to listen to what He communicates to our spirit and follow that.

Many miss the leading of God by following their own thoughts, following their own reasonings and their own mind, or by following their feelings and emotions.

Man is a threefold being. You are a spirit, you possess a soul (which consists of your mind, your will, and your emotions), and you live in a body.

God is a spirit, and when He communicates with you, He is going to communicate with you through your spirit. He doesn't communicate with you through your mind or your body. Now, what He says to your spirit will float up and enlighten your mind, but it doesn't originate from your mind, it comes from your spirit.

Romans 8:16 tells us, *"The Spirit itself* (Himself) *beareth witness with our SPIRIT...."* He bears witness with our spirit – not with our mind. When you need to know how He's leading you, look to your spirit, not your mind.

A Right of Sonship

"For as many as are led by the Spirit of God, they are the SONS of God" (Rom. 8:14). God is promising that as sons of God, He will lead us by His Spirit. The leading of the Spirit belongs to us as His sons – it's a right of sonship; this is His promise to us.

The leading of the Spirit doesn't belong only to those who are filled with the Holy Ghost with the evidence of speaking in other tongues, but it belongs to *all* of His sons; this is a right of sonship. We became His sons at the new birth. To be led of the Spirit is a right of the new birth; this is a promise belonging to *all* of His sons.

We don't *earn* the leading of the Spirit by praying or by reading our Bibles, for this *belongs* to us as sons of God as part of our birthright. Now, don't misunderstand me – we should read our Bibles and pray, for doing that will help us to develop our spirit and be more sensitive to the leading of the Spirit, but that doesn't *earn* us the leading of the Spirit, for God has made that ours as part of our birthright.

Defining the Spirit's Leading

God promises us that the sons of God are led by the Spirit of God. But many try to interpret for themselves what that leading of the Spirit is, and they get off.

Many think that the leading of the Spirit is to be led by a voice, a vision, a dream, or a prophecy. But nowhere in Scripture does God promise to lead us by any of these things.

Can one of these things happen? Yes. Can they be from God? Yes. But none of these are ways God *promises* to lead us.

In Romans eight, in the fourteenth verse, God promises to lead His sons by the Spirit of God. But in the sixteenth verse, we're told *how* the Spirit will lead us, "*The Spirit itself* (Himself) *BEARETH WITNESS WITH OUR SPIRIT....*" The leading of the Spirit that God is promising us is that the Spirit will *bear witness* with our spirit. He's not promising us a vision, a prophecy, a dream, or a voice. One of those things may happen, but they only happen as the Spirit wills; they are not promised to us.

What *is* promised is that the Spirit of God will *bear witness* with our spirit; we will have an *inward witness* in our spirit.

This is the *primary* way that God is going to lead all of His children. It is the safest way to be led, although it is not the most spectacular way God may lead.

It's more spectacular to hear a voice, have a dream, or see a vision, but that's not the primary way He leads because that's not the promised way He leads.

To hear a voice, have a dream, see a vision, or receive a prophecy, are all outward manifestations; therefore, the devil can duplicate all of them. The devil can cause you to hear a voice, he can give you a dream or a vision, or he can give you a false prophecy through someone. But because there's no devil in the spirit of the believer, he can never duplicate the inward witness; he can never bear witness with your spirit. That's why being led by the inward witness is the safest way to be led and why it's the primary way God leads all of His children.

The inward witness *trumps* every other leading. If you hear a voice, have a dream, see a vision, or are given a prophecy, *always* check your spirit. Does it bear witness with your spirit? Does it seem right to your spirit? If it doesn't, then reject it! I don't care who may have prophesied to you or how spectacular of a manifestation there may have been. The inward witness always trumps every other manifestation.

If someone gives you a prophecy, and it's from God, it will only *confirm* what you already have in your spirit. If what is said to you doesn't confirm what you already have in your spirit, then don't accept it; reject it. God doesn't use prophecy to lead you, but only to confirm what's in your spirit. Don't receive or act on what someone prophesies to you unless it bears witness with your spirit.

If God gives you a dream, a vision, or a prophecy, or if He speaks audibly to you, the inward witness will accompany it. That means if God does move by one of these more spectacular ways, it will always bear witness with your spirit that it's from God, *for the inward witness always accompanies any other leading from God.*

Chapter 3

The Inward Witness Defined

When the Spirit of God is leading you to do something through that inward witness, it will seem good to you, it will seem right in your spirit, it will seem to fit, you'll have a green light, or a "go-ahead" in your spirit – there will be a sense of peace in your spirit about doing it. That is the Spirit of God leading you to do it – follow that, obey that – that leading can be trusted.

It may not make sense to your head. Your head may even argue with it. Well-meaning loved ones may try to talk you out of it. But if you have peace about doing it, then ignore everything else and follow the leading that you have.

On the other hand, if the Spirit of God is leading you *not* to do something, you will sense a caution, a hesitancy, a grinding in your spirit, a red light, a dead feeling – you won't have peace in your spirit about it. That's the Spirit leading you not to do that. Obey that, follow that. *Never violate your spirit.*

Let Peace Make the Call

Isaiah 55:12 tells us, *"For ye shall go out with joy, and be LED forth with PEACE...."* The Spirit of God leads us through peace. You may not hear a voice from God, but if you have peace toward doing something, that is the Spirit of God leading you, and that's enough to act upon.

Now, there may be times you have peace in your spirit about doing something, but your mind is giving you fits. The peace that leads us is in our spirit, not our mind. Even if your mind is full of questions and doubts, just ignore your mind and follow the peace in your spirit, regardless of what your mind may be telling you.

Colossians 3:15 instructs us, *"And let the peace... from Christ rule (act as umpire continually) in your hearts [deciding and settling with finality all questions that arise in your minds]..."* (AMPC).

In a baseball game, the umpire makes the call in a play, and his call is final. Paul is telling us in this verse that the peace in your heart is to make the call, and what peace says is to be the final call. Don't let your mind, your emotions, or your feelings have the final call, but the peace in your heart is to make the final call – that's what you're to follow.

Peace Is the Clarity

Years ago, God began dealing with me about making a certain business transaction. I had peace in my heart about doing it, but my head was giving me fits. I had questions about it in my head, and my mind was racing with all kinds of thoughts regarding it.

Then I prayed a prayer that sounded real good, but it still wasn't a right prayer. I prayed, "God, I have peace in my heart about making this business decision, but my head is giving me fits. So, I'll tell You what I'm going to do; I'm going to spend time waiting before You until I get clarity on this." Sounds real good, doesn't it? But it still wasn't a right prayer.

So, for the next couple of weeks, I spent extra time waiting on God and praying in the Spirit about this business deal, but all the while, my mind was still giving me fits.

After a couple of weeks, God spoke to me about it. He said, "You told Me that you had peace in your spirit about doing this business deal, but because your mind was troubling you, you were going to wait before Me until you got clarity." Then God said to me, "The peace IS the clarity!"

In other words, the peace I had in my spirit was all the clarity I needed in order to act. God didn't answer all the questions I had in my mind; He just expected me to act on the peace in my spirit, regardless of the questions in my mind.

I made the decision to follow that peace and make that business deal, even though I had unanswered questions, and doing so blessed my life immeasurably.

The Inward Witness Is Supernatural

God was leading me by that inward witness to make that business deal, but because my mind was full of questions and unsettled, I was really looking for a more spectacular leading to help settle my mind. When I prayed that prayer, saying, "I'm going to wait before You until I get clarity," I was really saying that I wanted an additional leading other than the inward witness.

But God doesn't promise us an additional leading. He promises us that the Spirit will lead us by that inward witness. We have no scripture and no right to expect more. The inward witness is enough! It's enough to act on! It isn't as spectacular as hearing a voice, receiving a prophecy, or having a dream or vision, but it's still just as supernatural, for it comes from God. As my spiritual father often stated, "Many miss the supernatural by limiting God to the spectacular."

Many miss God and the leading of the Spirit by overlooking the inward witness. They want something more, and they miss the divine, supernatural leading of the inward witness.

The inward witness may be the only leading you ever get, for it is the only leading God promises us.

Many think that if something is life-threatening or there's danger involved, that God will warn them in a more spectacular and dramatic way. He may, but He may not. You can't count on that. We are to follow the inward witness. Be sensitive and obedient to follow that.

When we follow and act on that inward witness, we are following the Holy Spirit.

A Life Rescued

Years ago, a girl told me how God rescued her. She was to make a car trip with three of her friends. They had planned and saved money for a while to make the trip.

The morning they were to start the trip, she sensed in her spirit that she shouldn't go. She didn't know why, but she had the leading not to go. So, she listened to that.

When her friends came that morning to pick her up, she told them she couldn't go. They didn't understand why she wouldn't go, since they had been planning the trip for a long time. Even after much discussion, they still couldn't persuade her to go with them.

This is an important thing to note: don't let a sense of obligation sway you from following your spirit – *never violate or override your spirit!* Well-meaning loved ones and friends may try to persuade you in a particular direction, but don't override your spirit! They may even get upset with you. Let them get upset, but don't override your spirit!

Some may tell you that you should keep your word to them. We are to be people of our word. But if God warns us or corrects us, we should put what He says first; we should follow how He leads us and not override our spirit.

This girl's friends could not persuade her to go, so they made the trip without her.

The very next week, she came and told me the story. "Pastor, I refused to go with them on the trip. And on their way home, a big 18-wheeler truck hit their car head-on and killed all three of my friends."

Because she listened to her spirit and didn't override it, God was able to rescue her. It would have been easy for her to let her mind reason against the leading of the Spirit, but she didn't. She didn't know why the Spirit led her not to go. You don't have to know why the Spirit leads you to do something or not to do something. Just obey and follow that leading, and you'll be blessed.

Listen To Your Conscience

First Timothy 1:19 reads, *"Holding fast to faith...and having a good (clear) conscience. By rejecting and thrusting from them [their conscience], some individuals have made shipwreck of their faith"* (AMPC).

Your conscience is the voice of your spirit, and the believer is safe in following his conscience.

Paul told Timothy that some individuals had made shipwreck of their faith because they weren't following their conscience. If you follow your conscience, your faith will be protected and not shipwrecked.

What is your conscience telling you to do? Listen to that, and you'll be blessed. Don't reject and thrust from you your conscience by not following it. When someone doesn't follow their conscience, they don't follow what their spirit is saying to them, and they will face unnecessary difficulties and hardships. But if they listen to their conscience, they can avoid a lot of those difficulties.

As you sit in a church service listening to the sermon, your conscience may prompt you to address a particular change that is needed in your life. Don't ignore that, but follow it. While studying the Bible in your devotional time or spending time in prayer, your conscience may tell you of a change to make. Your conscience may speak to you to make changes spiritually, mentally (in your thought life), physically, or materially. Whatever arena your conscience tells you to make changes in, you'll be blessed when you obey that. If you ignore it, it can cost you much.

Now, don't allow yourself to get under condemnation and beat yourself up over anything of the past, or over faults, failures, or mistakes you've made, for your conscience won't accuse you or put you down; that's how the *devil* works. Your conscience will convict you, but never condemn you. Reject anything that condemns you, but follow the convictions of your conscience. Don't reject or thrust from you your conscience or override what it is saying to you. But listen to that; don't dismiss it. Obey what your conscience is telling you to do so that your faith won't be shipwrecked and difficulties will be avoided. Obeying your conscience will protect your faith from ruin.

Notice again what Paul stated in 1 Timothy 1:19, *"Holding fast to faith...and having a good (clear) conscience...."* A person of faith will follow their conscience. When people don't follow their conscience, it's a faith issue. Living a life of faith involves keeping your conscience clear by following its promptings.

The Assurance the Spirit Gives

Romans 8:16 reads, *"The Spirit itself* (Himself) *beareth witness with our spirit...."* The Amplified Classic translation reads, *"The Spirit Himself [thus] testifies together with our own spirit, [ASSURING US]...."*

When the Spirit of God is leading us, there's an assurance that comes with His leading. When He's leading us to go a particular direction, we're *sure* in our spirit that's the direction to go. We may not understand it all, and we may not be able to explain to others how we know it, but in our spirit there's an assurance that we're to go that direction. If He's leading us *not* to go a particular direction, there's an assurance in our spirit that we shouldn't go that direction.

Often times, someone decides what direction they want to go and then labels that as the leading of the Spirit. This is something you must be careful about.

Don't go to God regarding a matter having already decided what you're going to do. If you want to know the leading of the Spirit regarding a matter, you have to stay open to God. You have to be willing to hear what He may be saying to you and be willing to obey the inward witness.

Have that assurance in your spirit that the Spirit gives when He's leading. If you're not sure He's leading you in a particular direction, then don't do it.

Years ago, an individual told me that they were going to start a church. They didn't ask my counsel on it, they were just informing me of what they were going to do.

I sensed in my spirit they shouldn't do that, but they said God told them to do it. When they put that label on it, it closed the door for me to say anything different to them. But I knew that they had just decided this on their own, then labeled it as the leading of the Spirit.

Just a short time before they were scheduled to relocate to start the church, they said to me, "I hope we're doing the right thing."

I answered them, "I wouldn't make a move hoping it's right. You need to be sure."

Remember that when the Spirit is leading you, there's an assurance He gives – you're sure about it!

When that person stated, "I hope we're doing the right thing," they didn't have that assurance.

When the Spirit leads you in a particular direction, you may not fully understand everything about it, but you are *sure* you're to do it.

Some think they're acting in faith by moving blindly ahead, but faith doesn't move ahead blindly – it moves ahead with assurance – the assurance of the Word and the assurance that comes when the Spirit is directing and leading.

This individual made the move just hoping they were doing the right thing, but it never worked out, and they experienced great difficulties unnecessarily.

We must be careful that we don't make a decision and then label it as the leading of the Spirit. We must develop our spirit and learn to follow the inward witness, for that's the primary way He's going to lead us.

This individual, at one time, had much zeal to work for God, but zeal is not the leading of the Spirit. Being zealous about a plan *you've* made is not God's leading.

We must learn how He leads and become skillful in these things. That's when we'll experience the greatest success.

When Faith Is Easy

Faith is easy when you know the leading of the Spirit regarding a matter, because with the leading comes the assurance that the Spirit gives, and that assurance makes believing easy.

The Spirit will lead you regarding the right mate, the right local church to attend, the right job, the right house to buy, etc. When you know how He's leading, faith is easy, despite any challenges or opposition, because you have assurance in your spirit.

However, faith becomes a difficult thing when you aren't following the leading of the Spirit regarding a situation, because without the Spirit's leading, you'll lack the assurance of success. When you don't check your spirit to know the Spirit's leading, you are not assured that you're making right steps.

Be sensitive to the Spirit of God within. His leading and the assurance He gives causes your life of faith to be a joyous journey.

Chapter 4

It's Easy To Follow
the Spirit

I have heard many believers say, "God never speaks to me. I never hear God." Their problem is that they don't recognize how God speaks to them. They are expecting to hear a voice or have a feeling or some other manifestation.

The Spirit of God has been in them all along, endeavoring to lead them though that inward witness, but they have misunderstood or not recognized how He leads. Because they are expecting something else, they are missing the leading of the Spirit.

It is not hard to know what God is saying to you. It is not hard to know the leading of the Spirit. What you sense in your spirit, what that inward witness is leading you to do, is what God is saying to you. God doesn't often speak to us in an audible way or lead us in a spectacular way, but He always endeavors to lead us by His Spirit through that inward witness.

The devil would love for believers to think that it's hard to know what God is saying to them and what the Spirit is leading them to do. But it's not! The devil wants you to doubt your ability to hear from and follow God; he wants you to lose confidence in your ability to know God's leading yourself.

It's simply a matter of learning to recognize the Spirit, learning to recognize that He leads us through that inward witness.

So, we must take time to listen to our spirit. What's that inward witness leading you to do? What do you have peace about doing? What seems good to your spirit? That is God leading you. It's not hard to know the leading of the Spirit, but you will have to be sensitive to the Spirit to know His leading. Feeding on the Word, fellowshipping with God in prayer, and taking time to speak in other tongues will help you to be sensitive to the Spirit.

Jesus said, *"My sheep hear my voice, and I know them, and they follow me"* (John 10:27). Agree with Jesus. Agree with Him that you hear His voice and that you follow Him. He is leading you through that inward witness.

Don't say that you never hear God and don't know what He's leading you to do. His Spirit is in your spirit, and He's bearing witness with your spirit. Agree with God that He's leading and guiding you and that you do know His leading.

Many miss it because they're looking to their mind or feelings to know how God's leading them. But God doesn't lead us through our mind or feelings, but through our spirit. Proverbs 20:27 tells us, *"The spirit of man is the candle of the Lord…."* This simply means that God is going to enlighten us or lead us through our spirit, not our mind.

To know what the Lord is leading you to do in a particular situation, quiet your mind and check in your spirit; look to your spirit. What do you have peace about? Or what do you not have peace about? Follow that. That's the Spirit of God leading you through that inward witness.

Since God promised to lead all of His children by the Spirit of God, then it can't be hard to know the leading of the Spirit. It must be easy and simple enough for all of His children to do successfully. If it were difficult to know the leading of the Spirit, then many of God's children would fail, but God didn't implement a failing way to lead His children, but a successful way, for it's easy to know.

Don't Mingle the Mental with the Supernatural

When someone becomes confused when faced with a decision, it's usually because they've mixed the mental in with the spiritual; they've mixed their own human reasoning and thinking in with what their spirit is leading them to do.

What your spirit is leading you to do doesn't always make sense to your mind, so the mind will argue and struggle with what your spirit is leading you to do. You must learn to ignore what your head tells you if it's different than what your spirit is leading you to do. Never violate your spirit.

Hebrews 4:12 tells us, *"For the Word of God is quick* (alive)*, and powerful, and sharper than any twoedged sword, piercing even to the DIVIDING asunder of soul and spirit...."* Notice that the soul and spirit are to be divided, not mingled together. (The soul is the mind, the will, and the emotions.)

Since God leads us through our spirit and not our mind, people become confused when they try to know God's leading with their mind, or when they interject their human reasoning in with what their spirit is telling them, because they're mingling together what must be divided.

Divide the mental from the spiritual – don't mingle them. Learn to distinguish between what's coming from your spirit and what's coming from your mind.

It's not the leading of the Spirit that confuses people; rather, it's the mingling of the mind with the spirit that confuses them.

When making a decision, rather than just following what their spirit is leading them to do, they will make a list of pros and cons regarding their options. Even though they have the Spirit's leading, they think it's being responsible to list the pros and cons before making their decision. What are they doing? They are giving more credibility to what their mind can calculate than to the Spirit's leading. Then they wonder why they're confused. They're mingling the mental in with the spirit, and when they do that, they're not following the Spirit of God.

A Wrong Interpretation

Sometimes, people also become confused when they put their own mental interpretation on what the Spirit of God says to them or leads them to do.

God may speak to someone about something, and they put their own interpretation on it; then when it doesn't work out as they thought, they become confused. They knew God was dealing with them to do something, but again, they thought He meant something other than what He said, and they missed it.

One minister tells of the time that God dealt with him about his call. He had been pastoring, but God dealt with him that he was to have a traveling ministry instead. So this minister assumed that meant that he was called to be an evangelist. When he tried to go evangelize, he struggled, and things didn't work out well for him. When he asked God about the difficulties he was facing, God told him that he was struggling because he was trying to be an evangelist, when he was called to a different office altogether.

Just because God told him he wasn't a pastor, he assumed he was an evangelist; he put his own interpretation on what God was saying to him. When he did, he struggled. Yes, God was dealing with him all right about not pastoring any more – he got that part right. But when he put his own interpretation on what he thought God wanted him to do, he got that part wrong, and he began to struggle and become confused.

You can sense God dealing with you or leading you regarding something and get that part right. But if you put your own interpretation into some aspect of His dealing, you're going to get that part wrong, and it won't work out as God intended. Then you'll become confused because you thought God was leading you. He was leading up until the time you interjected your own thinking.

We need to rightly divide what God is telling us by not adding our own interpretation or human reasoning into it; then things will work out as God intended, and we won't become confused.

Spirit Dominated

As I stated, the soul and the spirit are to be divided, not mingled together. You need to be able to determine what comes from your soul (your mind, will, and emotions) and what comes from your spirit. Feeding on the Word will help you divide that because the Word is sharper than any two-edged sword, dividing between your soul and spirit.

As you feed on the Word and act on it, your mind will become renewed, and you'll begin to think in line with God's Word; you'll be able to more easily and clearly distinguish between your soul and spirit. You'll know how your spirit is leading you as opposed to following your soul, your own thinking and human reasoning.

We are to be dominated by our spirit and not by our soul. Those who live strictly out of their soul, dominated by their mind, will, and emotions, will never be as skillful as they could be in the things of the Spirit.

God gave us our mind, our will, and our emotions, but not for the purpose of dominating our life and leading us; that's the role of our spirit.

The Mind:

Those who are dominated by their mind will over-think things, run everything through their mind, and then follow their own mental reasonings. If it doesn't make sense to their mind, they won't accept it. That's why we're to live by faith, because the spirit of man can receive and believe what the mind cannot. But God doesn't lead us through our mind. Our mind is effective for handling many natural things, but the mind of man is not equipped or sufficient to take the lead in spiritual things. We must learn to ignore our mind when our spirit is leading us differently and follow our spirit instead of our mind.

The Will:

Those who are dominated by their human will are self-willed and very difficult for God, or anyone else, to lead. God doesn't override our will, for He gave our will to us. But we are to bring our will into agreement with His will for our life. We must practice this if we are to become skillful at following His Spirit.

The Emotions:

Those who are dominated by their emotions become very inconsistent in their life. They are up one minute and down the next, for emotions can rise or fall in an instant and with every changing circumstance. They become unsteady and unstable. They must practice not allowing their fluctuating emotions to dominate them, but allowing the Word to govern them.

We are to be dominated by our spirit, not our soul, for it is through our spirit that the Spirit of God will lead us.

A Disciplined Thought Life

We are to be dominated by our spirit and not by our mind, so we must learn to discipline our thought life. Satan's battleground is the mental arena. We can't keep Satan from bringing suggestions and troubling thoughts to our mind, but we can keep from entertaining those thoughts by refusing to turn them over and over in our mind. Christians must learn to discipline their thought life and not allow the thoughts and suggestions of the enemy to dominate their mind. It's difficult to know the leading of the Spirit when the mind is dominated by thoughts of fear, doubt, and worry.

Answer every wrong thought with the Word of God, then ignore the suggestions of the enemy. Those who don't discipline their mind will not be peaceful. You must discipline your thought life if you're to live in peace, for when you're in peace, that's when it will be easiest to know the leading of the Spirit.

Practice Following

If we are to be skillful in following the leading of the Spirit, we must *practice* following the Spirit. No one ever becomes skillful at anything without practice. Spiritual things, like natural things, must be practiced if we are to become skillful with them.

The Spirit of God will use everyday events and decisions to train us in following our spirit. He will use insignificant events of our daily life to practice spiritual things.

For example, you may be in a store intending to buy something, and the Spirit of God may check you, leading you not to buy it; don't override that – obey Him. No, it may not be a significant item you're intending to buy, but He will use the insignificant things of your daily life to train you in knowing and following His leading. What is He doing? He wants you to practice recognizing His leading and following it on insignificant things, so that when an important, significant event arises in your life, you will already be well acquainted with knowing His leading and skillful at following Him.

Agree With God

Some say they don't know what God is saying to them or that they're confused about what decision to make. Many times, they know in their spirit what they should do, but they don't *like* what they know. Since they don't like what they know, they don't want to acknowledge it. So, rather than acknowledging what they should do, they say that they don't know or that they are confused about what they should do.

The reason Christians struggle is because they haven't yet agreed with what the Spirit of God is leading them to do; they haven't agreed with what they know in their spirit. They try to reason and mentally convince themselves to go in a direction different than what they know in their spirit, and they can't, so they struggle.

The reason they haven't agreed to follow what they know in their spirit is because they're being self-willed – they are holding to what they want to do in that situation instead of agreeing with what they know in their spirit.

It's dangerous to be self-willed, for it can cost us much.

We can all look back at times in our life when we missed God and say, "I knew I shouldn't have done that. Something inside was telling me not to do that all along. I should have listened, but I didn't."

Listen to that leading inside. Listen to what you sense in your spirit; that's God's Spirit endeavoring to lead you. Don't violate that.

Through my 40 years in ministry, I have seen many people become self-willed, holding to what they wanted instead of agreeing with how God was leading them, and it cost them much. I have seen people get into wrong relationships, get into bad marriages, make bad business deals, make wrong moves, buy homes and properties they shouldn't have bought, take jobs they shouldn't have taken, and break fellowship with their pastor and local church. The effects of those self-willed decisions were devastating – leaving homes broken, families scattered, finances devastated, health ruined, relationships destroyed, and lives left on the spiritual junk heap.

We can't afford to become self-willed, and we shouldn't be unwilling or hard for God, or any man, to lead.

I've seen young people and middle-aged people get involved in relationships they knew they shouldn't be in, and the Spirit even dealt with them in an undeniable way not to get involved, but they did anyway. They reasoned in their mind against what they sensed in their spirit, and they were self-willed in wanting their way, and the result brought much difficulty.

Can God restore? Absolutely, He can! But it's just best to follow Him to begin with and avoid all of the difficulties.

In the past, there were times when I struggled and struggled against following what I sensed in my spirit to do, but when I finally obeyed, I realized that the struggle was far worse and much harder than the obedience. Once I obeyed, I was blessed, happy, and joyful; then I wished I wouldn't have struggled against it as I did!

To follow the Holy Spirit, you have to consecrate yourself to do the will of God instead of being self-willed. Jesus demonstrated His consecration as He prayed in the Garden of Gethsemane, *"...not what I will, but what You [will]"* (Mark 14:36, AMPC). That's how you consecrate yourself to

God – you commit yourself to yield to and carry out His will instead of your own. We are to consecrate ourselves to God's will all throughout our life.

When what God says is different than what you want, what are you going to do? Jesus didn't want to die, but He knew He must in order to carry out God's plan and will, so Jesus brought His will into agreement with God's will.

When what God says is different than what we want to do, what are we to do? We are to bring our will into agreement with His. Agree with God.

"Acquaint now yourself with Him [AGREE WITH GOD...]" (Job 22:21, AMPC). Notice what those who are acquainted with God do – they agree with God. Those who don't agree with God and struggle against what He leads them to do aren't as acquainted with God as they should be. If God leads you to do something, it's for your blessing and benefit; it's best for you. Those who know God know that.

If a young child is standing on a counter and a strong man who is a stranger to him holds out his hands and says, "Jump to me," the child will shake his head, "No," refusing to jump. But if the child's mother, who isn't near as strong, holds out her hands and tells the child to jump, he will joyfully leap forward into his mother's arms. Why? Because he knows her. He knows he is safe in doing what she says.

Likewise, when you know God, you jump when He says jump. Those who don't jump, don't know Him as they should.

Those who know Him know that what He leads them to do is for their own good, and it is always the safest and the best to follow and obey Him.

Again, Job 22:21 in the Amplified Classic translation reads, *"Acquaint now yourself with him [AGREE with God and SHOW YOURSELF to be conformed to His will]...."* To show yourself to be conformed to His will means to do His will, to obey Him. Some say they agree with God, but they aren't doing what He told them to do.

Over the years, there have been those who verbally agreed with things I said to them, even thanked me for what I said to them, but then they still went out and did what they wanted to do. They verbally agreed, but their actions said something different.

Some think that because they're courteous and agreeable to speak with that they are agreeing. It's the actions you take that demonstrate your agreement, not just the words you say and the agreeable tone you use.

In this verse in Job, we're told to show ourselves to be in agreement with God by what we do; we are to show our agreement through the actions we take.

JOB 22:21 (AMPC)
Acquaint now yourself with Him [AGREE with God and SHOW YOURSELF to be conformed to HIS WILL] and BE AT PEACE; by that [you shall PROSPER and GREAT] GOOD shall come to you.

When we bring our will into agreement with God's will and do what He says, we will be at peace, we will prosper, and great good shall come to us.

See the threefold reward of agreeing with God:

1) We will be at peace – there's no struggle.

2) We will prosper – our prosperity is connected to our obedience.

3) Great good shall come to us – not a small measure, but a great measure of good shall come. We won't have to chase it; it will come to us.

If we're going to be skillful in following the Spirit, we must bring ourselves into agreement with God's will for our life, for the Spirit leads us in line with God's will. We must agree with God in every arena of our life – spiritually, mentally, physically, and materially. When we agree with God and take steps to obey Him, the grace to accomplish what He tells us to do comes. The grace that enables us doesn't come until we agree, but once we agree, His grace always meets us.

Obey With Joy

There have been times when the Spirit of God has led me to do something I wouldn't have chosen to do on my own, so I not only had to bring my will into agreement with His will, but I also had to make sure I was obeying with joy, not with a grudge or grumbling, for only then could I be fully blessed in my obedience.

Isaiah 1:19 tells us, *"If ye be WILLING and OBEDIENT, ye shall eat the good of the land."* This verse tells us of a two-fold requirement to have God's best, to eat the good of the land – we not only have to be obedient, but we also have to be willing. This speaks to the attitude we are to have toward obeying Him.

God not only wants our actions of obedience, but He wants our heart to be willing, as well. He desires a heart that counts it a joy to obey Him. That's when we'll qualify to eat the good of the land.

Agree With Your Call

There are some called to the full-time, fivefold ministry who are struggling because they have yet to agree with what God is calling them to; they haven't agreed to the ministry, or they haven't agreed to the office they're called to.

The blessing is in the agreeing. The struggle is in the disagreeing. The struggling is far worse and much harder than the obedience. In the obedience is the blessing of God. So, agree with God and be at peace in every arena of life, and you'll prosper, and great good shall come to you.

Chapter 5

Immediately Obey Your Spirit

In following the leading of the Spirit, immediately obey and act on what He leads you to do. That's one thing that will help develop and mature your spirit more quickly because it causes you to become more spiritually sensitive to God.

Whatever the Spirit leads you to do, immediately respond to that. Those who respond more to Him will experience more of His leadings.

My husband, Dr. Ed Dufresne, made a statement years ago in line with this. He said, "The reason people don't receive more from God is because they don't respond more." The more you respond, the more you'll receive. People receive from God to the measure they respond to Him. You measure to yourself how much you receive based on how much you respond.

We can think back to school days and see that this is true. If we didn't pay attention to what the teacher said when we were in class, we didn't receive much from that class, and it was reflected in our grades. Just being present in the class didn't ensure us a passing grade. We had to respond to what was being taught and to what was going on in that classroom to succeed. We had to apply what we were learning when taking a test, or we would get a failing grade.

Well, there's the great Teacher on the inside of each of God's children – the Holy Spirit. But it's not enough that He's present within; we have to *respond* to that Teacher if we're to benefit from His Presence and His leading.

One of the primary ways we respond to Him is by immediately obeying what He leads us to do. Act on it without hesitation and delay, for the more we respond to His leading, the more we will receive.

We don't receive from God based on what's *in* us, but we receive based on what we *respond* to. To benefit from the Spirit within, we must listen to and obey Him in order to have success.

Now, there have been times that the Spirit of God showed me something that pertained to the future, but I knew I wasn't to act on it at that time. You'll know in your spirit if something He shows you is to be acted on later rather than immediately.

For example, God dealt with me about a home He had for us eight years prior to us getting it. When He started dealing with me about it, I knew it wasn't time for it yet; He was just letting me know about it so I would feed my faith for it and be ready to act on it when the time came.

But many things the Spirit leads us to do call for our prompt obedience.

Don't Mentally Analyze

Another great benefit of promptly obeying the leading of the Spirit is that it helps you keep the door closed to the devil. The enemy wants to draw you into the mental arena, for that's his arena. He wants you to mentally analyze what you sense in your spirit.

The leading you have in your spirit doesn't call for your mental analysis, but your prompt obedience. If you begin to mentally analyze what you have in your spirit, it will seldom make sense to your mind. And when you get in that mental arena, the devil will get you reasoning against the leading in your spirit and sway you from obeying your spirit.

To delay your obedience is to give the devil an opportunity to trouble your mind or for your mind to reason against the Spirit's leading.

The quicker you obey the Spirit's leading, the more peace you're going to experience, because you're not giving the devil an opportunity to trouble your mind and steal your peace.

Most of us have had God tell us to give money or an item to someone, and if we didn't give it quickly, we struggled with the thought of giving it. But once we gave it, the struggle stopped. Prompt obedience closes the door to the devil.

Chapter 6

Don't Get in a Ditch – Stay Balanced

Many Christians get off spiritually and become unsound when they try to be led regarding every little thing. They won't do anything, go anywhere, or help in any capacity unless they "feel led." You can take any truth to the extreme and get in the ditch. It's the same with trying to follow the Spirit of God; don't get into excesses that will cause you to become unsound and get in a ditch, but just stay in the middle of the road.

If the Spirit of God doesn't lead you in any particular direction regarding a matter, then just follow the knowledge you have. If the Spirit doesn't lead you differently, then evidently the knowledge you have is correct or enough for the situation. If the knowledge you have isn't sufficient or correct, that's when the Spirit will lead you differently than what your knowledge tells you to do.

For example, if you go to get in your car one morning and all four tires on your car are flat, you don't need the Spirit to lead you not to drive the car. Knowledge tells you that's dangerous. You don't need the Spirit to lead you. Act on the knowledge you have, for that knowledge is correct. When you follow the knowledge you have, you're still staying in line with God's will, even though the Spirit did not lead you specifically to not drive the car.

God gave you your mind. It's correct to follow the knowledge of your mind if the Spirit doesn't lead you otherwise. When it's wrong to follow your mind is when the Word or the Spirit leads you differently than what your mind is telling you to do.

When faced with a decision, large or small, if I don't sense a leading in a particular direction, I just use common sense or wisdom on what to do. Good judgment and common sense are important if the Spirit doesn't lead you a particular way. If I use good judgment and common sense when I don't sense a particular leading of the Spirit, then I'm still in line with God's will.

For example, it's common sense and good judgment not to leave a small child alone around water. We don't need the Spirit to lead us not to do that. Then if a child was to get hurt because they were left alone around water, we can't blame God for not leading us. God expects us to use good judgment and have common sense. We don't need the Spirit's leading regarding some matters.

A Good Deal

My spiritual father told of the time he was having a meal at his friend's home along with several others. His friend said, "Come with me, I want to show you something." They walked next door to another home. His friend showed him through the house and asked him if he liked it. When he said that he did, his friend said, "I own it, and I'll sell it to you at 1% interest."

My spiritual father stated, "I'll take it!" He said, "I didn't have to pray about it. I recognize a good deal when I see one."

He knew that he didn't have to wait for the Spirit to lead him to buy it – good sense told him to buy it. Now, if he shouldn't have, the Spirit of God would have checked him and cautioned him against it. But as he often stated, "You can go by what God *doesn't* say as much as by what He *does* say." In other words, if God doesn't tell you to go a particular direction, then do what is wise and makes good sense.

Red Lights Vs. Green Lights

I have found that God will more often check me in what *not* to do than tell me what *to* do. God leads more often by red lights than green lights.

When you're driving down the street, it's not the green lights that stop you, but the red ones. You just keep driving until you come up to a red light. That's the way it is much of the time in following God. Just keep going a particular direction unless He checks you or stops you. If He doesn't stop you, just keep going – that direction must be right.

Make Movement

Psalm 37:23 says, *"The STEPS of a good man are ORDERED by the Lord...."* Notice what God is able to order – a man's steps. If a man is taking steps, that means he's making movement in a particular direction. When he is moving in a direction, God can order his steps. But if a man won't even make a move, then God has nothing to order or direct.

Don't just sit back and wait for the leading of the Spirit before you'll make a move. Rather, move in the direction that wisdom or common sense would tell you to go, then if it's not right, God will check you and redirect you.

One important thing: don't go so fast in a particular direction and commit yourself in such a way that you couldn't back up if God checked you and redirected you.

Paul's Journey of Following the Spirit

ACTS 16:6-10
6 Now when they had gone throughout Phrygia and the region of Galatia, and were FORBIDDEN OF THE HOLY GHOST to preach the word in Asia,
7 After they were come to Mysia, they assayed to go into Bithynia: but THE SPIRIT SUFFERED THEM NOT.
8 And they passing by Mysia came down to Troas.
9 And a vision appeared to Paul in the night; There stood a man of Macedonia, and prayed

him, saying, COME OVER INTO MACEDONIA, and help us.
10 And after he had seen the vision, immediately we endeavoured to go into Macedonia, ASSUREDLY gathering that THE LORD HAD CALLED US for to preach the gospel unto them.

In this passage, we see that Paul made steps to preach in Asia, but the Spirit forbade him. He then made steps to preach in Bithynia, but the Spirit didn't allow him to do that either. After his attempts to preach in those two regions, then direction came as to where he was to go.

Notice that Paul didn't just sit in a house somewhere, refusing to move until the Spirit directed him as to where to go. Paul was taking steps, moving in a particular direction, and then the Spirit directed him to the right place. Because he was taking steps, the Spirit was able to direct him.

You can't steer a parked car – it has to be moving to be able to steer it. If you don't have a leading in a particular direction, then take steps to go in a direction that makes good sense and shows wisdom. If it's not the right direction, the Spirit will redirect you like He did Paul.

Faith makes movement – it doesn't sit stationary waiting for a leading. The Spirit's leading comes to those who are moving – not to those who are parked.

Paul didn't miss God by attempting to preach the Gospel in Asia and Bithynia, for when the Spirit forbade him, he obeyed the Spirit and did as he was directed, so he was still in the will of God.

You haven't missed God just because He redirects you; you miss God by not doing what He tells you to do.

"Buy This House!"

As I stated earlier, if you don't sense a leading in a particular direction, then follow the knowledge you have. Use good judgment, wisdom, and common sense, and then move ahead. You only need the leading of the Spirit if the knowledge you have isn't correct for that situation or if you don't have enough knowledge regarding the matter.

For example, my husband and I had our home up for sale, and we had gone one day to look at other houses on the market. When we walked into one particular home, the Spirit of God said to my husband, "Buy this home!" My husband said, "Okay, I will when our other house sells," but the Spirit said again, "No, buy this house now! Don't wait for the other one to sell."

Common sense and good judgment would tell you not to buy another home until you've sold your previous home, and that's what we would have done; that's the knowledge we would have acted on. But what the Spirit said trumped or superseded our knowledge and common sense. Since the Spirit said something different than our knowledge and our common sense, we obeyed the Spirit and went ahead and bought the other home. It wasn't too long after that that our previous home sold.

We didn't know that there were nine other offers that people had made to buy that home, but the Spirit knew it. If we hadn't bought it as quickly as we did, that home wouldn't have been available anymore by the time our previous home sold.

We didn't know enough about that home; we didn't have the knowledge the Spirit had about it, so that's why we didn't follow the knowledge *we* had. Rather, we followed the better knowledge the *Spirit* gave.

Follow Integrity

Proverbs 11:3 tells us, *"The integrity of the upright shall guide them...."* If you don't seem to have a particular leading of the Spirit in a matter, ask yourself, "What would integrity do?" Then follow that – when you follow integrity, that's what God would have you do.

Obey Bible Instruction

You don't need the leading of the Spirit when you have knowledge of what to do. When the Bible speaks to your need, you don't need the leading of the Spirit to do as the Bible instructs.

For example, you don't need to wait for the leading of the Spirit to tell you to give tithes and offerings to your local church. Malachi 3:8-10 instructs us to bring tithes and offerings to the storehouse. The storehouse is the place where our food supply is. For the believer, the local church is the storehouse. The local church is where our life and the lives of our family are fed. So, we should give tithes and offerings to our local church. We should also give offerings to other traveling ministries that feed our lives. We don't need the leading of the Spirit to be a doer of this Bible instruction. When you have Bible knowledge, you don't need the leading of the Spirit.

There may be something additional God wants you to give, so the Spirit may speak to you to give offerings to other ministries. He may speak to you to do that because that's in addition to the instruction the Word gives regarding the local church. If the Spirit leads you to do more, then obey Him.

Serving Doesn't Require a Leading

EPHESIANS 4:16
...the whole body fitly joined together and compacted by that which EVERY JOINT SUPPLIETH, according to the effectual working in the measure of every part, MAKETH INCREASE OF THE BODY unto the edifying of itself in love.

This passage is telling us that since we are all part of the Body of Christ, we all have a supply to bring to the Body; and when we all are doing our part, the Body works effectively, and the Body increases. The way that we bring our supply to the Body of Christ is by doing our part in the local church.

The local church is a family, and like a natural family, every member should be carrying out chores and bringing their supply to that family. If you don't, you're not functioning right in the Body of Christ. Those who bring a supply will receive a supply; those who don't bring a supply are not in a position to receive a supply. That's why many Christians have all kinds of difficulties in their life, because they aren't bringing their supply to the Body of Christ – they're out of joint. When a body part is out of joint, it doesn't work right.

Ephesians 4:12 tells us that the saints are to do the work of the ministry. It is the job of the pastor and the other fivefold ministers to teach the members of the Body so they can mature and know the supply they are to bring to the Body.

You don't need the leading of the Spirit to direct you to bring your supply and do your part in the Body of Christ. The Word instructs you to, and you are to act on that knowledge without even needing the leading of the Spirit.

In what capacity should you serve in your local church? Start with the area of your ability. What comes easy to you? Working with children? Mechanical projects? Technology? Music? Hospitality? Start with your abilities, but be willing to work anywhere you're needed; that's one way you bring a supply.

Some that are uncommitted and unfaithful will dismiss themselves from serving by saying God hasn't *led* them to serve. The Spirit doesn't need to lead you to serve when the Word has already instructed you to.

Let's stay in the middle of the road when it comes to following the Spirit. Let's give the Spirit's leading its proper place, but let's also give obedience to the instruction of the Word its proper place.

Chapter 7

Don't Wreck Your Faith

Faith works – but it's not for going *against* the leading of the Spirit. If the Spirit leads you to do something, you can't go in a direction that is against that leading and expect faith to work as it ought.

If you sense in your spirit to break off a relationship, to not take that job, to not buy that house or that car, etc., then don't override that. Your faith isn't so you can go against the leading of the Spirit.

Remember what Paul wrote to Timothy, "*...By rejecting and thrusting from them [their conscience], some individuals have made SHIPWRECK OF THEIR FAITH*" (1 Tim. 1:19, AMPC).

Your conscience is the voice of your spirit. If you sense in your spirit not to do something, but you do it anyway, you'll wreck your faith. Faith is not for going against your conscience.

For faith to work, you have to know the will of God regarding a situation. You can have faith for healing, you can have faith that God will provide for your needs, and you can have faith for all the promises of God, for His Word gives you the knowledge that that's His will. Faith works for the things that are in line with God's will – it's not for that which isn't His will for you. If the Spirit leads you to do something, then you can have faith for that. But if you go a direction different than where He leads, your faith won't work right.

Now, if you've missed God and gone against the leading of the Spirit, gone against that inward witness, then repent, and God will help you out of that situation. Your faith will work when you turn and go *with* God's leading and not *against* it.

When we go against, or override, the leading of the Spirit, God's not mad at us. He is just trying to spare us the unnecessary difficulties and hardships we'll face by overriding our spirit.

Be Someone Who Listens

One minister tells of the time he and his wife were in a restaurant with other pastors, and he ordered raw oysters. When the waiter brought them, the minister's wife said to him, "Those don't smell right. I wouldn't eat those if I were you."

"Oh, I'll pray over the food, and it will be all right." So, he prayed and ate the oysters.

Later that afternoon, he got sick with food poisoning. He asked God, "How come I got sick? I prayed."

God answered, "Your wife told you they didn't smell right, but you didn't listen, so you need to repent to her for not listening if you want to receive your healing." So he did, and he got better.

His wife told him not to eat those oysters, so he didn't need the Spirit to tell him; he should have listened to her. Wisdom was spoken to him, and even though he prayed in faith, his faith wouldn't work against that wisdom.

Now, if he was in a foreign land and had no other food to eat, then he could use his faith in prayer and claim that no deadly thing would hurt him, but that wasn't the case – he had a choice. His wife had the answer for him in her mouth.

We need to learn to recognize our help, even when it's spoken through the mouth of another person. Several times, I have had someone close to me say something that I recognized as my answer. It bore witness with my spirit, so I listened and didn't wait for God to speak further to me; I heard the Spirit's answer for me in the mouth of another.

If you're going to be led by the Spirit, you need to be willing to listen to someone who may have the Spirit's answer for you in their mouth, for even when it's spoken through someone, it will bear witness with your spirit.

Chapter 8

You Have an Unction

But ye have an unction from the Holy One, and ye know all things.

— 1 John 2:20

"BUT YE HAVE...." John is telling us something we already have, not something we're going to have when we get to Heaven, but what we have now as our present possession. It is ours to use now!

What do we have? *"But ye have an UNCTION...."* The word "unction" is the same as anointing, or the Holy Spirit; these are all synonymous terms, meaning the same thing: unction, anointing, the Holy Spirit.

This unction comes into the believer at the new birth; it is the anointing *within* every believer.

Now, there is an anointing that comes *upon* those in the fivefold ministry to empower them to fulfill their call; the anointing that comes *upon* can increase or decrease. We see that with Elisha, who asked for and received a double portion of the anointing that was upon Elijah (2 Kings 2:9).

But the anointing, the unction, that is within every believer doesn't increase or decrease; yet we can increase our sensitivities to that anointing within.

John said, *"But YE* (or you) *have an unction...."* Where is this unction, this anointing? It's in *you* – the real you – which is your spirit. It's not in your mind, and it's not in your flesh – it's in your spirit.

John tells us, *"But ye have an unction from the HOLY ONE...."* This unction doesn't come from any other source; it comes from God Himself.

What is this unction for? *"But ye have an unction from the Holy One, and YE KNOW ALL THINGS."* This unction, the anointing, the Holy Spirit, is in you so that you will know all things. What a tremendous statement. God wants us to know all things, so He gave us an unction.

This unction is not so that we'll know all things about plumbing, electricity, science, etc. *This unction is so that we will know all things pertinent to our life.* By the unction, the anointing, the Holy Spirit within, we can know what to do regarding every arena and every situation we face in our life.

Now, this unction won't cause us to know all things about our neighbor's life, but about our own life.

We are to know what to do when we're faced with a difficulty. God doesn't want us to go through life guessing, but knowing. *"...And ye KNOW all things."*

We won't know all things in our mind, for the unction isn't in our mind; it's in our spirit. We will know all things in our spirit. Then it is through that inward witness that the answer will be communicated to us. When we have the inward witness of what we're to do, then we know what to act on and what decisions to make.

Every born-again Christian has the unction in them to know all things. Then how come the lives of so many don't look like they know all things? Why do some seem to go from crisis to crisis with lives full of difficulty? Either they don't know to listen to their spirit, or they aren't sensitive to their spirit.

Your Answer Is Already in You

When my husband went home to be with the Lord in October of 2013, I was immediately thrust into a position of leadership and responsibility that was greater than before. I faced decisions that only I could make. There were many ministry, business, legal, and financial decisions to make. Each time I was faced with a decision, I didn't look to my mind, for my own understanding and education wasn't sufficient in those matters, but the unction, the anointing, the Holy Spirit, within me was more than enough. So, I would simply turn my attention to my spirit and check within for how the Spirit was leading me.

Because the unction to know all things was already in me, the answer to my need was already in me. I didn't have to ask God to send the answer down; it was already in my spirit. All I had to do was look to the inward witness to know what the unction, the Spirit within, was directing me to do. I didn't have to labor and spend long seasons in prayer to know the Spirit's leading, because the unction was already in me. I just had to quiet my mind and look within, and in a moment's time, I would always know by the inward witness what to do, for the answer was already in me.

You can develop your spirit so that you can instantly know what to do in all the affairs of life, for you have that unction within so that you'll know all things pertinent to your life.

Build in yourself the awareness of the unction in you. Throughout the day, say to yourself, "I have an unction in me to know all things." When you're faced with a decision, say to yourself, "I have an unction to know all things."

Quiet the Mind

Your spirit knows things your mind hasn't caught up with yet, so you will need to quiet your mind so you can hear what your spirit knows. A worried, troubled, fearful mind will cause you to miss the leading of the Spirit, but praising and worshipping God will help you to quiet your mind and draw up your answer from within.

Instead of worrying about situations you're facing, take time to worship and praise God. Thank Him that because the unction to know all things is in you, your answer is already in you, so there's no need to worry or fear.

As you take time to worship God and to rejoice, the answer from within will float up and enlighten your mind.

The answer is in your spirit, not your mind, so don't look in your mind for your answer. When packing for a trip, I've never yet gone to check the refrigerator to find my clothes – they're not there. Likewise, don't search your mind for God's answer to your need – it's not there. Look to your spirit; that's where you'll find your answer.

Because the mind is Satan's battleground, if you turn to your mind to try to find your answer, you will open the door to the devil to trouble your mind with fear, worry, or doubt. When Christians become worried or fearful, they are in the mental arena and have forgotten what's in them, in their spirit. They need to remember that they have an unction to help them know all things they need to know. Sometimes, the circumstances of life can look difficult, involved, tangled, and complicated, so people think their answer is complicated – but it's not. It's as simple as following the inward witness.

Don't become troubled by what your mind doesn't know; just walk in the light of what you do know, and what you need to know will be made known to you.

The Anointing Teaches You

First John 2:20 records what John stated, *"But ye have an unction from the Holy One, and ye know all things."* And just a few verses later, in verse 27, he states, *"But the anointing* (the unction) *which ye have received of him ABIDETH in you...."*

This anointing, this unction, abides in you; it doesn't come and go. It doesn't leave when you're facing difficulties; it's always within your spirit so you can access it anytime you need it.

John goes on to say in verse 27, *"...and ye need not that any man teach you...."* Don't misunderstand that verse. He's not saying that you don't need a pastor to teach you God's Word. Jesus gave apostles, prophets, evangelists, pastors, and teachers to the Body of Christ to help believers mature and grow up spiritually (Eph. 4:11&12). You need a pastor and the other fivefold offices to teach you God's Word. (When a man teaches under the anointing, that's not man teaching you, that's God teaching you through a man.) But there are specifics about your life that no man can teach you; only the Spirit can teach you those things.

God's Word is God's *general* instruction to all of His children, but there are *specifics* about your life that the Word doesn't give.

For example, God's Word tells you that He will supply all your needs, so you know He'll provide you with a home, but the Word doesn't tell you which home; you need the leading of the Spirit to know which home. God's Word lets you know what kind of a spouse to look for, but it doesn't tell you which one; the Spirit will lead you to the right one. God's Word instructs man to work a job, but the Spirit will lead you to the right one.

When the Spirit leads you regarding the specifics of your life, then you don't need to go to another man to ask him what to do; you just need to obey what the Spirit taught you to do, what He led you to do. That's what John was talking about in verse 27, *"But the anointing which ye have received of him abideth in you, and ye need not that any man teach you: but as THE SAME ANOINTING TEACHETH YOU OF ALL THINGS...."* The anointing, the Spirit within, will teach you what to do in every situation of life, so follow that.

It's The Truth & No Lie!

1 JOHN 2:27
But the anointing which ye have received of him abideth in you, and ye need not that any man teach you: but as the same anointing teacheth you of all things, AND IS TRUTH, AND IS NO LIE, and even as it hath taught you, ye shall abide in him.

When the Spirit leads you regarding what to do, it's the truth and no lie. It's not wrong; it's the right thing to do, for He always gives the right answer. He makes known to you the mind of God for your situation – it's the truth and no lie!

When you act on what He leads you to do, circumstances may not always line up immediately, so you may be tempted to doubt how the Spirit led you, but hold fast to what the

Spirit said and don't be swayed from that – it's the truth and no lie.

God told Moses to go tell Pharaoh, "Let my people go!" Even though Moses heard from God, Pharaoh didn't immediately comply. Instead, he increased the Hebrews' work load – things got worse for them. But what God said to Moses was "the truth and no lie," and as Pharaoh continued to oppose God's word, Moses continued to hold to it. Finally Pharaoh yielded. What if Moses had not held fast to what God said when it looked like it wasn't working and circumstances were getting worse instead of better? God's people would have stayed in bondage.

When the Spirit leads you to do something, remember, "It's the truth and no lie!" Stick with it! Hold fast to what the Spirit led you to do!

Several times, when I've acted on what the Spirit led me to do and nothing changed, but only got worse, I have just kept saying, "It's the truth and no lie! It's the truth and no lie!" And it would always turn out as the Spirit said.

If you're going to be led of the Spirit, you're going to have to be prepared to hold fast to what He leads you to do, in spite of all opposition. And when you do, the outcome will be just as the Spirit said!

The last phrase of 1 John 2:27 says, "...*and even as it* (the anointing) *hath taught you, YE SHALL ABIDE IN HIM.*" One meaning is that what the anointing, the Holy Spirit, tells you to do, stay with it and don't veer away from it. That is abiding in Him.

Following the Spirit will call for you to fight the good fight of faith, which is a fight of words. Keep saying the right words in the face of all opposition. Keep speaking what God's Word says, keep speaking what the Spirit led you to do.

The good fight of faith is a good fight because it's a winning fight. If you stay with what the Spirit said to do, you'll win – it's the truth and no lie!

Chapter 9

The Profit of the Spirit

But the manifestation of the Spirit is given to every man to profit withal.

– 1 Corinthians 12:7

This verse is introducing the nine gifts, or the nine manifestations, of the Spirit that are listed in the verses that follow. However, I want to look at this verse in a different light.

When any of the nine gifts of the Spirit are in manifestation, people profit from them. But *anything* the Spirit is involved in will profit. The Spirit of God is always connected to profit – never loss. Anytime there's loss or failure, either the Spirit wasn't involved, or He wasn't fully obeyed.

The Spirit's Involvement

The Spirit's involvement makes all the difference.

The Spirit of God was present at the time of Creation.

GENESIS 1:1-3
1   In the beginning God created the heaven and the earth.
2   And the earth was without form, and void; and darkness was upon the face of the deep. And the SPIRIT of God moved upon the face of the waters.
3   And God said, Let there be light: and there was light.

Why was the Spirit moving upon the face of the waters? He was in position, ready to move at God's words. *"And God said, Let there be light: and there was light."*

When God talks, things change. And the Spirit of God was present at Creation, moving and working to bring about that change. The Spirit's involvement brought about the change God spoke. Nothing was ever the same again because God spoke, and nothing was ever the same again because of the Spirit's involvement.

Set Free From a Habit

I can look back over the years and see the great profit I, and others, have experienced because of the Spirit's involvement.

Years ago, the Spirit of God moved upon me in a strong way to pray for someone who had been bound by the habit of smoking for over 40 years. They had tried to quit on their own many times, but had failed. After praying for them with the help of the Spirit for only five minutes, that person was set free. That person with a 40-year habit was set completely free after only five minutes of the Spirit's involvement. When the Spirit gets involved, things change. The Spirit's involvement in that situation made all the difference.

The key is to recognize and cooperate with the Spirit. When we follow His leading, we follow Him into changes needed, and there's profit.

I recognized when the Spirit moved upon me to pray for that person, and I cooperated with Him. When I did, the Spirit was able to bring about the change that brought profit.

Cooperate With the Spirit

"But the manifestation of the Spirit is GIVEN to every man to profit withal" (1 Cor. 12:7). Notice that the manifestation of the Spirit is *given*, not earned, or forced. Because it's given, what we must do is recognize when it's given and yield to it and cooperate with it.

"But the manifestation of the Spirit is given to EVERY MAN to profit withal."

Every man who cooperates with the Spirit will profit; every man who obeys and yields to the Spirit will profit. But the flip side of that is also true – every man who doesn't cooperate with the Spirit won't profit as he could.

God has profit in mind for us, not loss. But to experience the profit, we must learn to follow the Spirit.

My spiritual father had a vision of Jesus in which He said to him, "If you learn to follow My Spirit, I'll make you rich...." Following the Spirit will make us rich, cause us to profit. But it's conditional – we must learn to follow the Spirit. Every man who learns will profit; he'll profit from what he learns about the Spirit and from the Spirit.

The Spirit's help is for our profit, because all God wants us to experience is profit, never loss. Profit is what God has planned for us.

Many have experienced loss that could have been avoided if they would have cooperated with the profit the Spirit offered. When the Spirit leads us, He's offering us the opportunity to profit – not only financially, but in every way.

God began dealing with my husband and me in 1988 to relocate from Tulsa, Oklahoma, to Southern California. At the time, we had a church that sat on 85 acres which we needed to sell, but because it didn't sell immediately, we ended up staying in Tulsa another year and a half. But as we delayed making the move, the number of our road meetings began to decrease, and our finances began to dry up.

Finally, we made the move in 1990, even though the property hadn't sold. When we did, the property sold, but it took us another two years to begin to catch up financially.

We learned never to wait for property or possessions to give us permission to obey God. We experienced loss because we took too long to obey the leading of the Spirit; but when we obeyed, God turned our loss into profit.

Profit From the Spirit

"But the manifestation of the Spirit is given to every man to PROFIT withal."

If a business owner met with his store manager and asked to see a profit and loss statement, he would want to know what was gained and what was lost. If the manager was able to show a $50,000 profit for the month, he would be saying that the store had gained $50,000 more than it had before; it had money that it didn't have before.

When the Spirit causes us to profit, He will cause us to have what we didn't have before. We can have finances we never had before, but we can also have revelation, anointing, clarity, wisdom, understanding, knowledge, boldness, etc., that we never had before.

Profit Withal

"But the manifestation of the Spirit is given to every man to profit WITHAL." When looking in the dictionary for the meaning of the word "withal," I was surprised to learn that it means "in spite of." So, we could read this verse as, "The manifestation of the Spirit is given to every man to profit in spite of...in spite of the economy, in spite of opposition, in spite of circumstances, in spite of your upbringing, in spite of your lack of education, in spite of your surroundings, and in spite of what others may say."

When the Spirit is involved and obeyed, it doesn't matter what opposes, there's going to be profit.

A Reduction That Profits

In following the Spirit, sometimes He will lead you in a way that looks like it's reducing you instead of bringing profit, but if you'll just trust and follow His leading, the end result will be profit.

In the case of Gideon, who was leading God's people into battle against enemy armies that greatly outnumbered them, God had him send home those of his troops who were fearful. That day, 22,000 of his 32,000 soldiers turned back and went home; God was reducing them. Then after Gideon took his army of 10,000 to water to drink, God instructed Gideon to keep those who drank in a particular way, but said to send the others home. In fact, Gideon sent another 9,700 men home. God had reduced Gideon's army of 32,000 men to 300, and with those 300 men, they won a mighty victory.

It looked like God was reducing him, but He was really bringing him into increase. When following the Spirit, if it looks like He's reducing you, He's only bringing you into increase – you will profit.

Sacrifices That Pay

In 1990, when my husband and I finally relocated from Tulsa, Oklahoma, to Southern California, we sold our newly built church building that seated 1,000 people, along with the 85 acres it sat on, to follow the Spirit's leading. We sold everything we could to make the move and come to California, and we came with very limited funds. The move looked like God was reducing us, for we made many sacrifices to obey Him. But over time, that which looked like a reduction became our profit; we became more blessed in California, for that was where God led us. The increase didn't come overnight, but as we stayed faithful, the blessings increased.

Never step back from following where the Spirit leads you just because of sacrifices that will be called for. Those sacrifices may look like a reducing, but they will turn to your profit, for every man who follows the Spirit will profit.

Practice Listening

To follow the Spirit, you have to be teachable and be willing to be led. To be someone who is good at following the Holy Spirit, you have to be willing to be led, and you have to practice following. The best way to become skillful at following the Holy Spirit who you *can't* see, is to be skillful at listening to and following those that God puts in your life who you *can* see. Listen to those who have a voice of authority in your life: your spouse, your pastor, your employer, etc.

Those who don't listen will argue, talk back, and be self-willed. They are more practiced at *not* following. But someone who is willing to be led will listen to others when they should and follow as they should; they will be practiced at following and will be more likely to follow the leadings of the Spirit.

We must be people who listen if we're to be led into profit by the Spirit of God.

We have all failed to listen to and follow the Spirit as we should have at sometime in our life. When we did, we suffered loss for it and faced unnecessary difficulties, but hopefully, we learned our lesson.

Anyone who has failed to listen or missed the Spirit's leading can repent and start listening to and following the Spirit. When they do, God will turn their loss into profit, for He has profit in mind for us, and following His Spirit will bring us into it.

Chapter 10

The Advantage the Spirit Gives

But now I go my way to him that sent me; and none of you asketh me, Whither goest thou?

But because I have said these things unto you, sorrow hath filled your heart.

Nevertheless I tell you the truth; It is expedient for you that I go away: for if I go not away, the Comforter will not come unto you; but if I depart, I will send him unto you.

— John 16:5-7

When Jesus was on the earth, the lives of the disciples and those around Him were dramatically different. To hear Him, to follow Him, and to see what God did through Him caused their lives to leave the ordinary and the mundane and move into the supernatural and the extraordinary. To be in His Presence meant their lives would never be the same again.

However, on this day that John records, everything began to change for them; Jesus announced something they had never expected – He would be leaving.

Then He made another dramatic statement, telling them that it was *expedient* (advantageous) for them that He go away. How could that be? How could it be expedient for them for Him to be absent rather than present?

Jesus was telling them that it was to their *advantage* for Him to go away and to send the Comforter, the Holy Spirit. To have the Holy Spirit is to have the advantage; to have the Spirit within would give them the advantage in every situation in their life.

When Jesus was on the earth, He could only be *with* these disciples, but when the Comforter, the Holy Spirit, came, He would be *in* them.

Everything that Jesus was to them, the Holy Spirit would be to them, but more, since He would indwell them and lead and guide them. This most certainly would be expedient for them – it would be to their advantage.

In John 16, John goes on to record how expedient and advantageous it would be for them when the Holy Spirit came.

> **JOHN 16:12-15**
> **12 I have yet many things to say unto you, but ye cannot bear them now.**
> **13 Howbeit when he, the Spirit of truth, is come, HE WILL GUIDE YOU INTO ALL TRUTH: for he**

shall not speak of himself; but whatsoever he shall hear, that shall he speak: and HE WILL SHEW YOU THINGS TO COME.
14 He shall glorify me: for he shall receive of mine, and SHALL SHEW IT UNTO YOU.
15 All things that the Father hath are mine: therefore said I, that he shall take of mine, and SHALL SHEW IT UNTO YOU.

The Holy Spirit within them would guide them into all truth. God's Word is the truth He would guide them into. God's Word is God's will. God's will is seen in His Word. The Spirit would guide them into the truth of God's Word and God's will. The Spirit of God would take of God's will and show it unto them.

Only those who know the truth and know God's will can carry it out and fulfill it. The Holy Spirit would make that known to them.

How expedient or advantageous to know the truth and the will of God concerning the matters of life! That gives us the advantage in life.

First Corinthians 2:11 tells us, *"...the things of God knoweth no man, but the Spirit of God."* The will of God, the plan of God, and the mind of God are known by the Spirit of God. The Spirit knows the mind of God and God's will for our life.

Verse 12 goes on to tell us, *"Now we have received, not the spirit of the world, but the spirit which is of God; that we might know the things that are freely given to us of God."*

We need the Spirit's help to even know and comprehend all the things that God has provided for us and made ours.

As one minister stated, "God planned it, Jesus purchased it, but the Spirit leads us into it." We need the Spirit's help to unveil and lead us into what God planned and what Jesus purchased for us. Apart from the Spirit, we would never be able to explore, know, and comprehend to the fullest all that God has made ours.

This helps us to see why Jesus told the disciples that it was expedient, or to their advantage, that He go away, so He could send the Holy Spirit to them.

What Jesus told the disciples came to pass on the Day of Pentecost when the Holy Spirit came in as a mighty rushing wind and filled them all (Acts 2:1-4). He had come to show them all that God had provided and to lead and guide them into it.

But to benefit from His leading, we must learn to recognize how He leads, then follow Him closely – not veering from His leading – for those who follow best finish best. Our finish will be determined by how well we follow.

The Spirit's Counsel Gives the Advantage

As we follow Him, He will guide us in our daily affairs. We don't have to live by trial and error, but we can know God's will and God's mind on matters we face.

When my husband moved to Heaven in October of 2013, my life changed dramatically. Not only was I thrust into another level of leadership, but I had many ministry, business, and legal matters to now oversee and complete.

At the time of my husband's home-going, there were several important business projects he had started that I had to complete – building construction to finish, property matters to resolve, and several other pressing projects.

I remember one occasion in particular when I was on a conference call with several lawyers and other businessmen, trying to resolve a business matter. We were not agreeing on some details, and some of them were trying to pressure me into making decisions I didn't think were right. I excused myself from the room, then walked into my office and said to God, "What do You say I should do?" Then I quieted my mind and turned to my spirit. The Holy Spirit within witnessed to my spirit, "Stand firm." When I sensed that, I then had the mind of God on the matter – I knew what to do. I didn't know what to do because I had a legal education or a business background, but I knew what to do because I had higher counsel than anyone else in the meeting – I had the counsel of the Holy Spirit, who made known to me the mind of God in the matter.

I walked back into that meeting with something – the advantage! I walked back in there with the advantage the Spirit gave me when He made known to me the mind of God. The others were operating out of *their* mind, but now I was operating out of God's mind, for the Spirit gave me God's thoughts on the matter.

Did they immediately welcome the final decision I gave them when I walked back in? No, not all of them. But that didn't matter to me. I knew to hold fast to what God had said in spite of that. As I held to the counsel the Spirit had given, it was eventually resolved correctly. Oh yes, there was a fight from some, but the fight of faith was easy for me as I stood my ground, for I had the assurance that came from knowing the Spirit was leading me.

I've had to face several legal, financial, and business matters since that time, but even though I don't have a legal, financial, or business education like those I have encountered, I have still faced them with the advantage, for I had the counsel of the Genius inside – the Holy Spirit who made known to me the mind of God.

But in those times, I also knew something else. I knew how to stand immovable in the face of opposition. When you have the counsel of the Spirit, the leading of the Spirit, the inward witness in a matter, you have to know "it's the truth and no lie" (1 John 2:27). Don't allow *any* opposition to sway you or make you question or doubt that inward witness, for it's the truth and no lie. The Spirit's leading is worthy of complete obedience and honor. We honor the Holy Spirit by obeying His leading, no matter what the circumstances and opposition.

You don't have to be the most educated person, but you do need to learn to recognize and follow the Spirit, the inward witness, and stand your ground, refusing to be swayed. Remember this – when you follow the Spirit's leading, you have the advantage!

Chapter 11

Your Measure of Faith

Romans 12:3 tells us that, *"...God hath dealt to every man the measure of faith."* The beginning measure of the faith of God is given to every man at the new birth; that same measure is given to each man.

It is then up to each man to cause that measure of faith to grow. By feeding and acting on the Word of God, faith is increased. But if a man neglects his faith, his faith will decrease. It's important that we feed our faith on God's Word and act on that Word so our faith will continue to grow, for, *"...faith cometh by hearing, and hearing by the word of God"* (Rom. 10:17).

Each man has a different measure of faith according to how much he has fed his faith, and when the Spirit of God leads, He will lead every man within *his* measure of faith, never beyond it.

When someone tries to believe or act beyond his measure of faith, he will fail, but if he stays within his measure, success will come.

Since the Spirit of God is always connected to profit, He will never lead in a way that will cause someone to experience loss; He will always lead someone within their measure of faith.

Following Requires Faith

However, when the Spirit does lead in a particular direction, the route He leads will require faith. So, if the outcome is to be successful, and if we're to profit, we must use our faith.

When God delivered the Hebrews from slavery in Egypt, He led them in the route they were to take. One place He led them to was the wilderness. It should have only been a short journey through the wilderness, but because they refused to believe God, acting in unbelief instead of staying in faith, they stayed in the wilderness for 40 years. They lingered in a place they were only meant to pass through. Why? They didn't use their faith, but instead acted in unbelief.

If you're going to follow the Spirit and move with Him, you're going to have to operate in faith. If you're going to profit from His leading, you must stay in faith.

A Personal Experience

Years ago, I was having some physical issues, and the doctor prescribed some medication for me, but I didn't want to take it. I was thinking wrong then, for I thought if I took the medication, that meant that I didn't have faith, and I knew that if I was going to receive my healing from God, I was going to have to stay in faith. I was having such a struggle about it.

My husband helped me correct my thinking by telling me that it's not the withholding of medicine that pleases God, but faith. So, I saw that someone can withhold medicine, but that doesn't necessarily mean they have faith to receive from God, or that someone can take medicine and still exercise their faith.

It was a few days later that the Spirit of God spoke to me about what to do. He said, "Go on the medication, but while you're on it, continue to feed and exercise your faith. When your faith grows to the measure you need, then I'll tell you when to come off the medication."

So, I went on the medication, but I also daily fed and exercised my faith. A short time later, the Spirit of God spoke to me again, "You can come off the medication now, but keep exercising your faith." So I did, and all of my symptoms left. It was easy for me, because my faith had grown and I had stayed within my measure of faith, so I received my answer.

The Spirit of God knows your measure of faith, and He will always counsel and lead you in line with your measure of faith, for that's the only way you'll have success.

Because the Spirit leads people based on their measure of faith, He will lead different people differently. He will lead one person to go to the doctor, and He will lead another one not to go to the doctor. No matter what He leads a person to do, they must still exercise their measure of faith. He will not lead them in a way that doesn't require them to use their faith.

He doesn't lead a person to go the medical route so they won't have to use their faith. He directs them to go the medical route while they are feeding and increasing their faith so that their faith can continue to grow to where it needs to be.

Now, just because you may not *want* to go the medical route doesn't mean you have the measure of faith to not go the medical route. Again, follow that inward witness, for the Spirit will always lead you the right way.

Don't Overextend Your Faith

When purchasing a home or any large item, it's especially important to be sensitive to the Spirit's leading, because He will lead you in line with your measure of faith so you don't overextend yourself financially or overextend your faith.

It's one thing to have enough faith for the down payment on a home, but it's a whole other thing to have enough faith to maintain the cost of the home every month.

There have been some who have purchased a home with enough income to support it, but they didn't have the measure of faith to support it. Then when their income decreased, their measure of faith wasn't sufficient to support it, and they struggled. In some cases, they ended up losing their home.

Just because someone may want something doesn't mean they have the measure of faith to support it. Always stay within your measure of faith.

Just because someone may want something doesn't mean the Spirit is leading them to get it. Always be sensitive to how the Spirit is leading, for then when you do get something, it will bless you and not become a difficulty for you.

Some people get adamant about buying something or about going a particular direction, but being adamant is not the same as having faith. Don't let your own adamancy or the adamancy of a loved one cause you not to be sensitive to or disregard the leading of the Spirit. He will lead you in line with your measure of faith, for He knows what you can believe for.

If there's something you want, but you realize you may not yet have the measure of faith to support it, that doesn't mean you can't have it. That simply means you must take the time to feed and increase your faith so your faith grows to the appropriate measure.

But always know this: the Spirit leads you within your measure of faith, for that's the safest place for you to be.

How To Know Your Measure of Faith

Romans 15:13 shows us how we can know our measure of faith. *"Now the God of hope fill you with all JOY and PEACE in believing...."* When you are believing within your measure of faith, you'll be in joy and peace, even in the midst of pressing or difficult circumstances.

If you're not in joy or peace, then you're out beyond your measure of faith. Get back within your measure of faith. It's not doubt and unbelief to back up to get within your measure of faith.

If you receive a bill for $10,000 unexpectedly, and you become overwhelmed and troubled at the thought of believing God for the $10,000, then you're out beyond your measure of faith, for you're not in peace and joy. At what level do you not seem overwhelmed or troubled? Can you believe for $1,000 easily? Is that where you have peace and joy? Then believe for $1,000 ten times. Believe for $1,000, and then when that comes, believe for another $1,000. Then keep at it until you have the entire $10,000. When you're within your measure of faith, what you're believing for will come more easily.

Do you have a lot of debt? Don't try to believe for the entire sum to be paid at once. Break it down into smaller amounts that you can believe for, and believe for one portion at a time.

When you stay within your measure of faith, that's when you'll have success. Don't allow the devil, circumstances, or well-meaning loved ones pressure you to extend yourself beyond your measure of faith; stay within the measure where you have peace and joy.

Be sober about the measure of faith you have, for the Spirit will lead you within that measure.

Chapter 12

Ministering by the Spirit

Just as I follow the inward witness in my daily life, I follow the inward witness when ministering in a service.

Prior to a service, I check my spirit to know which direction to go in the service. I look to my spirit to know what message to teach. I don't need a spectacular leading; I just dip down in my spirit to see what seems good to me. There will be a subject that seems to fit, so I simply go that direction. Usually, it's something God has been dealing with me about. I recognize that He's usually dealing with me along a particular line because I need it and because the people I minister to need it. I don't seek to preach on some random topic; I just identify what He's been dealing with me about and follow that.

If no particular topic seems to stand out to me, either He will give it to me when I get in the pulpit and I'll teach by revelation, or He wants to do something altogether different in a service where I may not teach at all, but flow with the Spirit.

One important thing my husband taught me about ministering is this: *if you don't sense a leading in any particular direction, just go with the first thing that comes to you when you get in the pulpit – whether it's a revelation to teach or a gift of the Spirit that goes into operation – follow that.*

Before a service, I may sense that I'm to minister by the gifts of the Spirit after I teach (1 Cor. 12:7-11). If I sense that, I don't turn to the mental arena to try and figure out or mentally plan what to do; I just quiet my mind and don't touch it in my thought life. Then I let the Spirit lead me when I'm in the service.

If you go to the mental arena to try to figure out what or how you're to minister by the Spirit, you can open yourself up to the devil, because the mental arena is his arena. Either your mind will conjure up something, or the devil will suggest something to do, and you may think that's the leading of the Spirit, and you'll get off.

If you sense that God wants to move by His Spirit, don't touch it in your thought life. Instead, quiet the mind, and know that He'll lead you when you're in the service.

Now, I know that sometimes God will show you beforehand what you're to do in that service – you may know exactly the flow of the Spirit that God wants. That's fine, but that knowing still will come to you from your spirit and not because you turned to the mental arena to formulate a plan.

It Takes Faith To Follow the Spirit

Many ministers step back from yielding to the flow of the Spirit in services because in following the Spirit, they won't know everything in advance; it will be shown to them as they need it.

There's an element of mystery when following the Spirit because you won't know everything – He'll only show you what you need to know when you need to know it, and the natural mind doesn't like that.

It requires faith to follow the Spirit and to flow with the gifts of the Spirit. If a minister is more developed in following their mind rather than their spirit, they will become fearful and draw back from the move of the Spirit.

Don't Yield to Fear

We all have to make sure we're not drawing back in some way.

Some ministers' wives, and others God wants to use in a greater way, step back from preaching, teaching, or flowing with the Spirit, because they get in the mental arena and become fearful at the thought of God using them. They get in the mental arena about it, and when they do, they open the door to the devil, and fear comes in, so they draw back.

If God deals with you about ministering, just stay out of the mental arena about it and hook up to your spirit. You'll find that God will fill your mouth and people will be blessed.

Signs Following

When ministering, we are to dip down into our spirit and draw on what's within, then we are able to tap into a greater flow that blesses the people.

When I'm finished teaching in a service, I always pause and check my spirit to see if there's something more God wants to do by the Spirit. I don't assume I'm done when the teaching's done. God may want to confirm the Word preached with signs following (Mark 16:20), so I always give opportunity for that to happen. No one can make that happen, for that happens as the Spirit wills, not as we will, but we should be sensitive to the Spirit if He wants to move that way.

If God does want me to minister further by the gifts of the Spirit, I will have the inward witness to do that.

So in looking to my spirit, I won't necessarily have a dramatic leading, but I may sense that I'm to minister to someone with a particular physical condition or in some other way, so I just call that out.

The gifts of the Spirit operate in line with the inward witness. I just follow what I sense and what seems right to my spirit, and I call those things out.

Now, since I endeavor to follow the inward witness in my daily life, then I'm already practiced when it comes to following the inward witness in a service and ministering by the gifts of the Spirit. If a minister isn't sensitive to the Spirit in his daily life, it's likely he won't be in a service, either.

Obey God in the Gifts

My husband was very keen in following the Holy Spirit, and many of us learned much from him.

One of the things he taught me was if a minister persists in missing and bypassing the leading of the Spirit and does not yield to the gifts or the move of the Spirit in a service, it can open the door to difficulties for him.

God has a plan for every service, and ministers must develop their spirit so they will be keen to the Spirit's leading; they should know and cooperate with God's plan for the services they conduct.

God's plan is God's will. If a minister repeatedly misses God's plan for services, he won't fulfill God's will, and when he's out of the will of God, he opens the door for the enemy to attack him.

My spiritual father told of the time he started having physical problems because God had told him to hold Holy Ghost meetings, and he didn't move as quickly with that as he should have, so he opened the door for the devil to attack him. He made the correction and obeyed God, and as a result, his physical symptoms left and he also became an example to many ministers of how to flow with the Spirit.

Without his obedience, many ministers would have had no example. That's why it was so critical for him to conduct those meetings.

God had told him, "If you don't teach My people how to flow with the Spirit, there will be a whole generation who won't know the move of the Spirit."

We can see then the importance of following God's plan for our services, for so much is connected to our obedience.

Some ministers have had health problems because they persistently missed the leading of the Spirit in their services. After they would preach or teach, the anointing would come to minister by the Spirit, but instead of yielding to that, they would close the service and dismiss without the Spirit getting to manifest as He wanted.

It's important to preach and teach the Word, but it's also important to allow the Holy Spirit to have His way so that the people can profit from the manifestation of the Spirit.

The Move of the Spirit Blesses

Some ministers may say that a move of the Spirit will run people off, but the genuine move of the Spirit blesses people, for it meets their needs; it doesn't run them off.

What will turn someone off is when people try to force or conjure up a flow that isn't the Spirit, but the flesh. That's why we must learn the move of the Spirit and flow skillfully and with excellence – not draw back from it.

Knowing the Genuine From the False

As I stated in chapter two, the devil can imitate some of the ways God moves. The devil can give someone a dream or a vision, or speak in an audible voice. But the devil will also seek to imitate the nine gifts, or manifestations of the Spirit, spoken of in 1 Corinthians 12:7-10.

As a minister, always check with your spirit when operating in these gifts. Does the operation of these bear witness with your spirit?

The flow of these gifts will come from your spirit and float up to enlighten your mind, but they will not originate from your mind.

When the devil seeks to imitate these gifts, they will come to your mind and not from your spirit.

Since these manifestations of the Spirit operate as God wills, and not as man wills, if a minister tries to force these manifestations of the Spirit, he can open himself up to a familiar spirit. A familiar spirit seeks to imitate the Holy Spirit.

You will know the genuine from the false by the inward witness.

Take Time To Learn

If we are to learn, we must be students of those who know the move of the Spirit and who set a sound example for us to follow.

There are some ministers who will never fulfill all God has for them unless they take time to be in services to receive from those ministers who know how to follow the Spirit, for many of these things are learned and caught through associations, demonstrations, and impartations.

If a minister has lost skill at flowing with the Spirit in his services, he should get around those who do flow with the Spirit. He will catch something from them, and it will enhance his ministry.

However, many ministers are too busy to be in the services they should be in so they can learn; that will cost them much. We must make sure these things are a priority to us and make time to sit under those who know; our ministries depend on it.

Chapter 13

Developing Your Spirit

When we take the time to develop our spirit, we will be more sensitive to the leading of the Holy Spirit.

There are four steps you can take to develop your spirit:

1) Meditate on the Word

2) Practice the Word

3) Give the Word first place

4) Instantly obey the voice of your spirit

#1 – Meditate on the Word

To meditate on the Word means to mutter it to yourself and to think deeply into it. Take a verse of scripture that seems to speak to you, then mutter it repeatedly to yourself and think deeply into its meaning.

For example, you could take the verse in 1 John 2:20 that I've referred to and meditate on it. It says, *"But ye have an unction from the Holy One, and ye know all things."* Repeat that over and over to yourself as you go about your day – as you ride in your car, as you work around the house, as you lay in bed at night. Say to yourself, "I have an unction, an anointing from God, that helps me to know all things pertinent to my life. I always know what to do in every situation, for I look to and follow the anointing within."

As you do that, it will make you more aware of and turn your attention to the truth of that verse. Then when you're faced with a decision, you'll already know what to do – you'll look to and follow the unction within that's leading you.

You have to take time to make the Word real to you. Meditating on the Word is what makes the Word real and makes it come alive to you. Until it's real to you, you won't benefit from it as you should.

Meditation is how you put the Word in you and how you put you in the Word – that's how you make it real and make it come alive to you.

JOSHUA 1:8
This BOOK of the law (the Word) **shall not depart out of THY mouth; but THOU shalt meditate THEREIN** (in the Word) **day and night, that thou mayest observe to do according to all that is written THEREIN** (in the Word)**: for then THOU shalt make thy way prosperous, and then THOU shalt have good success.**

God is telling us how to have success. We are to do two things: we are to meditate on the Word day and night (it's to be a lifestyle), and we are to do it, act on it. When we get the

Word in us (in our spirit and in our mind) through meditating on it, and we do it in every arena of our life, success is sure.

In recording the verse, I capitalized the words I wanted you to see. The "Word," in some form, is referred to three times. "You," in some form, is referred to five times. God is not referred to, and the devil is not referred to. Since "you" and the "Word" are what is referred to, your success in life is determined by what *you* do with the *Word*! Your success isn't determined by God, and your lack of success isn't determined by the devil. Your total success is determined by what you do with the Word. To improve or to have greater success, you're going to have to do more with the Word – which means more meditating and more doing.

If we're to develop our spirit, we must meditate on the Word.

#2 – Practice the Word

The verse we just looked at in Joshua 1:8 included the instruction to meditate on the Word and to do it, practice it. The value of meditating on the Word is that it then directs your actions.

It's not enough to know what the Word says, or even be able to quote it, unless you're going to practice it. It's not enough to go to a good church, sit under a good pastor, or say "amen" to the sermon and shout about it, unless you're going to do it. Knowing people who do the Word won't make you successful; you have to do the Word for yourself.

People deceive themselves into thinking they're spiritual just because they know what the Word says, but it's the *doing* of the Word that determines one's spirituality.

James 1:22-25 tells us that it's the doer of the Word that's blessed, not the hearer only, and that the one who hears the Word, but doesn't do it, will forget it and not live up to who God made him to be.

To keep our faith alive, we must be doers of the Word. Faith will die without the "doing" of the Word. *"Even so faith, if it hath not WORKS* (actions of faith), *is DEAD, being alone* (not accompanied with corresponding actions)" (James 2:17).

We are not saved by works (by doing works to earn our salvation), but once we're saved, works are everything! For without works (the doing of the Word), faith is dead. One day we will all stand before Jesus to give an account of the things we have done in this life, whether good or bad (2 Cor. 5:10); therefore, works matter!

If we're to develop our spirit, we must be doers of the Word – we must practice the Word in every arena of life – it must become our lifestyle.

#3 – Give the Word First Place

In every circumstance of life, we must learn to put the Word first. When faced with a difficulty, we must learn to ask ourselves, "What does the Word say?" Other well-meaning people may give us their advice, but it's what the Word says that is most important.

Put what the Word says before what others say and before what your mind may say, and act on that; that's how you put the Word first, and that's what will help develop your spirit.

#4 – Instantly Obey the Voice of Your Spirit

The Spirit of God communicates God's will to your human spirit, so when you follow your spirit, you are following the Holy Spirit.

What the Spirit conveys to your spirit is worthy of obedience. Faith will instantly obey, but doubt will delay obedience.

What your spirit tells you to do is safe to obey, and by instantly obeying your spirit, you will develop your spirit.

Being Sensitive to the Spirit

We can develop our spirit and become so sensitive to our spirit that we can know instantly what the Spirit's leading is in a situation. Because God promises to lead His children by the inward witness, the leading of the Spirit belongs to us; therefore, we don't have to labor and pray for long seasons to know how He leads. We are to just become sensitive to His leading, for He is present within to lead us.

Keep the Flesh Under

Those who are sensitive to the Spirit are not ruled and dominated by their flesh; they keep their flesh under the dominion of their spirit.

Romans 8:14 tells us, *"For as many as are led by the Spirit of God, they are the sons of God."* But the verse right before that, verse 13, tells us, *"For if ye live after the flesh, ye shall die: but if ye through the Spirit do mortify the deeds of the body, ye shall live."*

It's interesting to note that mortifying (abstaining from, and disciplining) the deeds of the flesh is spoken of directly before God's promise to lead us.

To be sensitive to the Spirit's leading, we have to deal with the flesh; we must discipline it and keep it under the dominion of our spirit.

Paul stated in 1 Corinthians 9:27, *"But I keep under my body, and bring it into subjection: lest by any means, when I have preached to others, I myself should be a castaway* (set aside as unusable).*"*

Paul stated that he had to keep his body from dominating his life by making it subject to his spirit – he let his spirit dominate him instead of his flesh.

If a man's body is left without restraint and dominates him, his body will lead him into ruin. We are not to yield to our body, but to our spirit. We do that by obeying and following our spirit, rather than yielding to the desires of the body.

We also keep from yielding to our body by guarding and disciplining our mind, holding it on the Word and off the desires of the flesh.

We have the help of the Holy Spirit in keeping the flesh under so that our spirit dominates us instead of our flesh. The Holy Spirit empowers us, as we follow our spirit, to keep our flesh under.

Speaking in Tongues Keeps the Flesh Under

Again, Romans 8:13 tells us, "...*ye through the Spirit do mortify the deeds of the body....*" As we yield to the Spirit, He empowers us to keep our flesh under. One way we yield to the Spirit is by speaking in other tongues.

Praying in the Spirit, in other tongues, helps keep the body under the dominion of our spirit, for speaking in tongues builds up our spirit so that our spirit is stronger, and we are fortified to keep the flesh under.

Those who spend time to speak in other tongues daily will cause their spirit to be more sensitive to the Holy Spirit, for their flesh won't be dominating them. The more sensitive we are to the leading of the Spirit, the more of the Spirit's leading we will experience.

Chapter 14

Following the Spirit Regarding...

In this chapter, I will touch on following the Spirit regarding several different things without dedicating an entire chapter to each of them individually.

The topics touched on will be following the Spirit regarding:

1) What to believe for
2) Healing
3) Finances
4) The will of God
5) Prayer

#1 – Following the Spirit Regarding What To Believe For

Look to the Spirit's counsel before you set your faith on some things.

Years ago, God began dealing with me that He had another house for us, but I didn't start looking at the time He started dealing with me, for I sensed it was several years away. I was right, for we didn't find the house until six years later, and it was over two years after that before we moved into it.

At the time we found the house, we weren't actually looking; someone just took us to see the new house that had been built next door to them. But when we walked inside it, my spirit got excited.

That night, after everyone else was in bed, I started talking to God about that house.

I knew God had another home for us, and I really liked that house. But I also knew that faith works, and if I set my faith on something, I could get it, even though it might not be God's highest and best for me. So I wanted God's counsel on it before I set my faith on it. Was this the house He had planned for us?

While I was talking to Him about it, He dealt with me in an unusual way, and I knew it was the home He had for us. (I later saw that the reason He dealt with me in such a unique way was because we encountered much opposition in getting into the home, and dealing with me in that supernatural way helped hold me steady in faith during that time.)

But as I stated, when we were walking through the home, my spirit was excited. I had the inward witness that this was the home He had for us. That would have been enough to act on if He hadn't dealt with me in a more dramatic way.

Especially when making a big decision, make sure you follow the leading of the Spirit so you know what to set your faith on. Don't just set your faith in some random direction or on some random thing. Before you set your faith, look to the inward witness to know the Spirit's leading.

2 – Following the Spirit Regarding Healing

When in need of healing, we have a right to claim it, for that's one of the things God has provided for us.

But if symptoms persist, look to the Spirit for His counsel and to receive God's wisdom. John 16 tells us that He will lead us into all truth. Proverbs 4:7 tells us that, *"Wisdom is the principal thing; therefore get wisdom...."* God will give us the wisdom we lack if we will ask in faith (James 1:5), then we'll know what to do in the face of difficulties.

Years ago, my husband was diagnosed with cancer that had spread to all of his lymph nodes, and his condition was quite serious.

When we came home from the doctor's office after hearing the diagnosis, he talked to God about it. He said, "Alright God, where have I missed it? I know You don't miss it, so I must have."

God spoke back to him, "There are two areas you haven't obeyed Me in. Number one, you haven't been resting like I told you to do two years ago. Oh yes, you changed for a while, but then you went back to your old habit of not resting enough.

"Number two, you haven't obeyed Me as you should in the prophet's office. I tell you to say something, and you don't because of the opposition that may come."

When Ed heard those things from God, he immediately repented and made the corrections, and then God spoke to him again, "Okay, the cancer will all be gone within 30 days." And when he went back to the doctor 29 days later, the doctor said to him, "Somebody up there must really like you, because it's all gone!"

Ed did receive some kind of treatment during that time, but it wasn't supposed to produce the result that he got. His healing was, no doubt, supernatural.

What I wanted you to see is the importance of looking to the counsel and leading of the Spirit and the wisdom He gives when in need of healing, for He knows the answer to your need. He may lead you to a particular verse to stand on, or He may tell you of changes to make, like He did with Ed. Just be sensitive to anything He may deal with you about. But if He doesn't deal with you about anything specific, you can just boldly take your stand on the healing Word, for healing belongs to us.

#3 – Following the Spirit Regarding Finances

Just as with healing, prosperity belongs to you. So if you run into financial difficulty, you have a right to stand on God's Word to provide for you. But if your answer is delayed in coming, look to the Spirit to show you if something more needs to be addressed; He will show you.

Prosperity is not simply about the money or possessions you have – prosperity is a way of thinking. Sometimes, you may need to correct something in the way you think. If that's the case, the Spirit will show you the needed corrections; He will make known to you the wisdom of God for your situation.

If there is strife in your home, in your marriage, or with some other person, that will affect your finances.

But the truth is, there are numerous things that will affect your finances, so look to the Spirit's leading to know if any corrections or other actions need to be taken.

As Jesus stated to my spiritual father, "If you learn to follow My Spirit, I'll make you rich...."

When I've gone into some poverty-ridden nations and taught on prosperity, some people just looked at me, seemingly unable to grasp what I was talking about. All around them was poverty, all they saw was poverty, and lack was the flow of their surroundings, so it seemed to be difficult for them to grasp the thought of prosperity and reach for it.

In contrast, because I was raised in the United States and have traveled to many countries, I've seen great wealth and prosperity. I've seen it, and I know it's available and possible.

Well, since the Holy Spirit is from Heaven, He has seen the great riches, supply, and provision of Heaven – He has been a participant in the great economy of Heaven, which has no lack, but only abundance and unlimited resources. He has seen far greater wealth than we have ever seen.

Having seen some of the wealth and supply of the United States, I long for those in nations with great poverty to reach for more, for I know so much more is available and possible.

Well, likewise, the Holy Spirit, who has seen Heaven's great wealth, and who is a participant in the surpassing wealth and supply of Heaven, looks at us and our life with great longing; He longs for us to reach for more, for He knows all that has been made available to us and what's possible. But it's difficult for some to grasp, for we limit ourselves to what we see around us. But if we will follow the Spirit, He will lead us into the wealth and abounding resources *He* sees.

The Word tells us that Jesus was made poor that we might be made rich (2 Cor. 8:9). At Calvary, not only were our sin and sickness laid on Him, but so was poverty; that's when He became poor.

Ephesians 1:3 tells us that, *"...(God) hath blessed us with all spiritual blessings in heavenly places in Christ."* One translation reads that, "God has blessed us with everything that heaven itself enjoys." That's what the Spirit is endeavoring to lead us into.

God spoke to my husband years ago and said, "Ninety-seven percent of My people are living beneath what I've provided for them." We must renew our mind with the Word and feed our faith so we can move into what God has provided for us. But we must also develop our spirit so that we're sensitive to the Holy Spirit, who is endeavoring to lead us to reach beyond the limitations of earth and into the resources Heaven has made ours.

#4 – Following the Spirit To Know God's Will

EPHESIANS 2:10 (AMPC)
For we are God's [own] handiwork (His workmanship), recreated in Christ Jesus, [born anew] that we may do those good works which God predestined (planned beforehand) for us [TAKING PATHS WHICH HE PREPARED AHEAD OF TIME], THAT WE SHOULD WALK IN THEM [living the good life which He prearranged and made ready for us to live].

God has a plan for each of our lives, and as we follow the paths He has for us, we will fulfill His will, as well as "live the good life."

God created that plan for us, but the Spirit reveals and leads us into that plan.

1 CORINTHIANS 2:9 & 10
9   But as it is written, Eye hath not seen, nor ear heard, neither have entered into the heart of man, the things which God hath prepared for them that love him.
10 But GOD HATH REVEALED THEM UNTO US BY HIS SPIRIT: FOR THE SPIRIT SEARCHETH ALL THINGS, yea, the deep things of God.

The Spirit plays a role in revealing to us God's will for our life, and when we follow Him, He will lead us into the fulfillment of God's will.

Jesus stated in John 4:34, "*...My meat is to DO THE WILL OF HIM that sent me, and to FINISH HIS WORK.*"

Jesus was saying that as meat nourishes and sustains the body, so the will of God was to His life – that's what nourished and sustained Him. And He didn't intend to just start God's will, but to finish it as well.

It's carrying out the will of God for our life that causes us to be fully nourished and sustained, yet we need the Spirit's help in knowing that plan.

Anytime the Spirit leads us in a particular direction, it's always in harmony with God's plan, never in opposition to it.

He will lead us to take a step in a particular direction. At the time, we might not realize how many other things will be connected to that step and have a domino effect on future events.

Romans 8:26 tells us, "*...the Spirit itself* (Himself) *maketh intercession for us with groanings which cannot be uttered* (in your articulate speech)." This verse is referring to praying in other tongues. The Spirit makes intercession for us as we pray in other tongues.

Romans 8:27 tells us, "*...he* (the Spirit) *maketh intercession for the saints ACCORDING TO THE WILL OF GOD.*"

Since we don't understand what we're saying when we're praying in tongues, this verse assures us that the utterances in tongues the Spirit gives us are "according to the will of God"; they're always in line with God's will.

When you need to know God's will in a matter, the Holy Spirit will lead you into the understanding of God's will as you pray in other tongues.

The Holy Spirit knows the will of God for you, and since the Holy Spirit is in your spirit, the will of God is in your spirit. And as you take time to speak in other tongues, you tap into and access the will of God.

If I could say it this way, the will of God is like a puzzle; when you open the box, all the pieces are there, but they're not in place.

Likewise, the plan of God is in your spirit; all the pieces of God's will are there, but they're not yet in place. As you come into each new season of your life, certain pieces are called for. As you take time to pray in the Spirit and follow the leading of the Spirit, the pieces you need are accessed from your spirit and put in place in your life, and then more of the picture of God's will for your life comes into view.

The puzzle isn't put together all at once – it takes a lifetime of faithfulness and obedience to the Word and the Spirit for the picture of God's will to be complete. But as we daily walk in the light of the plan of God, we will "live the good life."

As we pray in the Spirit, it's like laying a railroad track so that the train of God's will can move further ahead. The more we take time to pray in the Spirit, the more track we lay, and the further God's will can move forward.

If we seem to be behind in the plan of God, we can catch up if we will take time to pray more in the Spirit; for the more we pray, the faster and further God's will can move forward.

#5 – Following the Inward Witness in Prayer

Sometimes, you may sense the anointing to pray come on you. The devil doesn't want you to yield to that, for he's the one who suffers from it the most, but if you will respond to it, it will bring great blessing to someone or to a situation.

Sometimes, you may sense in your spirit that you're praying for a particular person, but don't let your mind "fill in the blanks." If the Spirit doesn't give you clarity on it, then you don't need it.

Simply quiet your mind, putting it in neutral, and focus on your spirit.

In an attempt to stop or distract you from praying, the devil will suggest all kinds of things to your mind to try to hold you in the mental arena and out of the faith arena, the spirit arena.

When my children were young and I was traveling on the road, at times a strong burden to pray would come on me. Immediately, the devil would suggest to my mind that something was wrong with one of my boys, and the thought of it would try to trouble me. The devil was trying to hold me in the mental arena and out of the arena of faith, the spirit arena. He did not want me yielding to the Spirit in prayer.

But as I grew spiritually, I learned to recognize this strategy of the enemy. I learned to quiet my mind and not allow it to follow any troubling thoughts, but to focus on my spirit and yield to the spirit of prayer until it lifted.

Know this – anything God may say to you as you pray will come from your spirit; always follow the inward witness when praying. Don't let any strategy of the enemy against your mind during that time make you fearful or troubled.

When praying in the spirit, in other tongues, you may never know what you're praying about, but you don't need to know to be effective.

If you need to know what you're praying about, you will know that by the inward witness, so don't put your own mental interpretation on it.

Chapter 15

In Closing

The Holy Spirit endeavors to lead every believer through the inward witness, but because many haven't recognized His leading or don't know to follow the inward witness, they face difficulties unnecessarily.

Becoming skillful in following the Holy Spirit won't happen overnight, but as we practice it daily, we can live the life God intended for us.

God not only wants every believer to know the leading of the Spirit, but He also wants the entire Body of Christ to develop in these things.

In this era, God is raising up strong local churches that flow with the Word and the Spirit. God is raising up a people who will be keen and skillful in the things of the Spirit and move with Him to fulfill His great plan in the earth. We cannot accomplish this apart from the help of the Holy Spirit; He is our great Helper in this.

As we follow the Word and the Spirit, it will be as Daniel stated, *"...the people that do know their God shall be strong, and do exploits"* (Dan. 11:32).

Prayer of Salvation

Heavenly Father, I come to You in the Name of Jesus. Your Word says, *"...him that cometh to me I will in no wise cast out"* (John 6:37). So I know You won't cast me out, but You will take me in, and I thank You for it.

You said in Your Word, *"...If thou shalt confess with thy mouth the Lord Jesus, and shalt believe in thine heart that God hath raised him from the dead, thou shalt be saved. For whosoever shall call upon the name of the Lord shall be saved"* (Rom. 10:9 & 13).

I believe in my heart that Jesus Christ is the Son of God. I believe Jesus died for my sins and was raised from the dead so I can be in right-standing with God. I am calling upon His Name, the Name of Jesus, so I know, Father, that You save me now.

Your Word says, *"...with the heart man believeth unto righteousness; and with the mouth confession is made unto salvation"* (Rom. 10:10). I do believe with my heart, and I confess Jesus now as my Lord. Therefore, I am saved! Thank You, Father.

Please write us and let us know that you have just been born again. When you write, ask to receive our salvation booklets.

To contact us, please email us at
dm@dufresneministries.org
or write to:
Dufresne Ministries
P.O. Box 1010
Murrieta, CA 92564

How To Be Filled With the Holy Spirit

Acts 2:38 reads, *"...Repent, and be baptized every one of you in the name of Jesus Christ for the remission of sins, and ye shall receive the GIFT of the Holy Ghost."* The Holy Ghost is a gift that belongs to each one of God's people. Jesus is the gift God gave the whole world, but the Holy Spirit is a gift that belongs only to God's people.

Jesus told His disciples, *"But ye shall receive POWER, after that the Holy Ghost is come upon you: and ye shall be witnesses unto me..."* (Acts 1:8). When you're baptized with the Holy Spirit, you receive supernatural power that enables you to live victoriously.

Indwelling vs. Infilling

When you're born again, you receive the indwelling of the Person of the Holy Spirit. Romans 8:16 tells us, *"The Spirit itself* (Himself) *beareth witness with our spirit, that we are the children of God."* When you're born again, you know it because the Spirit bears witness with your own spirit that you are a child of God; He confirms it to you. He's able to bear witness with your spirit because He's in you; you are *indwelt* by the Spirit of God.

But the Word of God speaks of another experience subsequent to the new birth that belongs to every believer, and that is to be baptized with the Holy Spirit, or to receive the *infilling* of the Holy Spirit.

God wants you to be full and overflowing with the Spirit. Being filled with the Spirit is likened to being full of water. Just because you had one drink of water doesn't mean you're full of water. At the new birth, you received the indwelling of the Spirit – a drink of water. But now God wants you to be filled to overflowing – be filled with His Spirit, baptized with the Holy Ghost.

> **ACTS 2:1-4**
> **1   And when the day of Pentecost was fully come, they were all with one accord in one place.**
> **2   And suddenly there came a sound from heaven as of a rushing mighty wind, and it filled all the house where they were sitting.**
> **3   And there appeared unto them cloven tongues like as of fire, and it sat upon each of them.**
> **4   And they were all FILLED with the Holy Ghost, and BEGAN TO SPEAK WITH OTHER TONGUES, as the Spirit gave them utterance.**

When these disciples were filled with the Holy Ghost, they began to speak with other tongues as the Spirit gave them utterance; they spoke in a language unknown to them. Today, when a believer is filled with the Holy Ghost, they will speak with other tongues too. These are not words that come from the mind of man, but they are words given by the Holy

Spirit; these words float up from their spirit within, and the person then speaks those out.

What is the benefit of being filled with the Holy Ghost with the evidence of speaking in other tongues? First Corinthians 14:2 reads, *"For he that speaketh in an unknown tongue speaketh not unto men, but unto God...."* When you're speaking in other tongues, you're speaking to God – it is a divine means of communicating with your Heavenly Father. This is one of many great benefits.

> **MATTHEW 7:7-11**
> **7 Ask, and it shall be given you...**
> **8 FOR EVERY ONE THAT ASKETH RECEIVETH...**
> **9 ...what man is there of you, whom if his son ask bread, will he give him a stone?**
> **10 Or if he ask a fish, will he give him a serpent?**
> **11 If ye then, being evil, know how to give good gifts unto your children, HOW MUCH MORE SHALL YOUR FATHER WHICH IS IN HEAVEN GIVE GOOD THINGS TO THEM THAT ASK HIM?**

In this passage, Jesus is saying that when you ask God for something, you shall receive it! Believe that He will give you that which you ask for. When you ask God for something good, He won't give you something that will harm you; He will give you the good thing you ask for. The baptism of the Holy Spirit is a good gift, and when you ask God to fill you with the Holy Spirit, you won't receive a wrong spirit; you will receive this good gift, the gift of the Holy Spirit.

Once you receive the gift of the Holy Ghost, you can yield to this gift any time, speaking in other tongues as often as you choose; you don't have to wait for God to move on you. The more you speak in other tongues, the more you will benefit from this gift. By continuing to speak in other tongues on a daily basis, you will be able to maintain a Spirit-filled life; you will live full of the Spirit.

The more you take time to speak in other tongues, the deeper you'll move into the things of God.

(For more teaching on being filled with the Holy Spirit, I recommend the mini-book, *Why Tongues?* by Kenneth E. Hagin.)

Prayer To Receive
the Holy Spirit

"Father, I see that the gift of the Holy Spirit belongs to Your children. So, I come to You to receive this gift. I received my salvation by faith, so I receive the gift of the Holy Spirit by faith. I believe I receive the Holy Spirit now! Since I'm filled with the Holy Spirit now, I expect to speak in other tongues as the Spirit gives me utterance, just like those in Acts 2 on the Day of Pentecost. Thank You for filling me with the Holy Ghost."

Now, words that the Spirit of God gives you will float up from your spirit. You are the one who must open your mouth and speak those words out. The words will not come to your mind, but they will float up from your spirit. Speak those out freely.